MW01125406

THE HEALING POWER OF THE HOLY COMMUNION

ALSO BY JOSEPH PRINCE

Eat Your Way to Life and Health
No More Mind Games
Anchored
Live the Let-Go Life
Thoughts for Let-Go Living
The Prayer of Protection
The Prayer of Protection Devotional
Grace Revolution
Glorious Grace
The Power of Right Believing
100 Days of Right Believing
Unmerited Favor
100 Days of Favor
Destined to Reign
Destined to Reign Devotional
Healing Promises
Provision Promises
Health and Wholeness Through the Holy Communion
A Life Worth Living
The Benjamin Generation
Your Miracle Is in Your Mouth
Right Place Right Time
Spiritual Warfare

For more information on these books and other inspiring resources, visit JosephPrince.com.

JOSEPH PRINCE

THE HEALING POWER OF THE HOLY COMMUNION

A 90-DAY DEVOTIONAL

Published in Nashville, Tennessee, by Emanate Books, an imprint of Thomas Nelson. Emanate Books and Thomas Nelson are registered trademarks of HarperCollins Christian Publishing, Inc.

Cover design by 22 Media Pte Ltd.

Thomas Nelson titles may be purchased in bulk for educational, business, fund-raising, or sales promotional use. For information, please e-mail SpecialMarkets@ThomasNelson.com.

All emphases in Scripture quotations and testimonies were added by the author.

ISBN 978-0-7852-2944-5 (eBook)
ISBN 978-0-7852-2943-8 (HC)

Library of Congress Control Number: 2019956958

Printed in the United States of America

20 21 22 23 24 LSC 10 9 8 7 6 5 4 3 2 1

CONTENTS

BEFORE YOU BEGIN

Did you know you can ask God for a long, good, and healthy life? Are you aware that God is still healing people today? And have you ever wondered if it is the will of God for you to be healed or whether you qualify for His healing power?

I don't know what circumstances you are confronted with today. Perhaps you or your loved one has been diagnosed with a critical illness, and you are still reeling from shock, fear, and helplessness. Or maybe you suffer from a condition and you have resigned yourself to it being "God's will."

My friend, whatever situation you might be faced with, do not give up. Not now. Not ever. No matter how dire your medical report might be, God can still turn your situation around. He is a God of miracles, and whatever giant you might be faced with today, He is bigger.

Your outward circumstances might be discouraging, but you know what? You can see these things, and that means they are *temporal*. The Bible tells us that "the things which are seen are temporary, but the things which are not seen are eternal" (2 Cor. 4:18).

There is an enemy who uses the visible to snare you and oppress you with fear and discouragement. But I believe the Lord arranged for you to be reading this book because He wants you to keep your eyes on Him—the invisible God who is eternal. He will never leave you nor forsake you. You have a God who loves you so much He gave His own life for you on the cross.

And yet people have somehow believed the lie that sometimes it is God's will for us to be sick. There are even those who claim that God uses sickness to "chastise" us or teach us a lesson. These lies have robbed His people of partaking of their blood-bought right to divine health and caused many believers to simply accept sickness in their bodies.

My friend, God is *not* the author of sickness, disease, and death, and He never intended for man to suffer from them. The destructive power of disease and death was released into the world through an act of eating when Adam and Eve ate from the Tree of Knowledge of Good and Evil. Adam sinned against God, and the wages of sin is death (Rom. 6:23).

The good news is, our beautiful Savior didn't just die for our sins—He also paid the price for the healing of our sicknesses and diseases with His own body. And because of His work on the cross, we can believe for healing and divine health. The Bible declares that "by His stripes we are healed" (Isa. 53:5).

How can we receive this provision of health and wholeness? Just as death and sickness came through the act of eating, I believe God has ordained that another act of eating reverses the curse of sin and releases life, health, and healing. In other words, *you can eat your way to life and health.*

What am I talking about? I am talking about the holy Communion.

The truths behind the holy Communion have been by and large neglected by the body of Christ, with many seeing it as a mere ritual or tradition and partaking of it only a few times a year, or at most once a month. But because of the revelations God has unlocked for our church, we have been partaking of the holy Communion every Sunday for close to two decades. As a result of the preaching of the gospel of grace as well as how God has ordained the holy Communion as a channel of receiving healing, health, and wholeness, I have received healing testimonies from people all around the world. I cannot wait to share some of them with you in this book.

Interestingly, many people think the way to live a long and healthy life is to watch what they eat and exercise. Don't get me wrong. By all means eat well, stay away from excesses that will damage your body, and choose the right exercise program. But our dependence cannot be on diets, fancy activity trackers, exercise apps, and health foods. Thank God for nutritionists and fitness instructors. They are fighting the same battle. Our trust, however, has to be in the redemption purchased by Christ and not in creation.

Divine health and long life can only come from God. His provision for life and health is not sold in a bottle, nor is it a plan or a pill. It has been given to us freely, but it came at an astronomically high price that was paid on the cross of Calvary by the Son of God Himself.

HOW TO USE THIS DEVOTIONAL

This collection of ninety daily devotionals contains excerpts from my book *Eat Your Way to Life and Health* that will help guide you to receive—through partaking of the holy Communion—the full benefits of all the Lord Jesus has purchased for you. I want you to know beyond the shadow of a doubt that God wants you healed, whole, and well. I want you to know that God's heart is for you to enjoy a long, healthy, and satisfying life.

The Healing Power of the Holy Communion is divided into twelve sections. Each section uncovers faith-building truths from the Bible about the healing power of the holy Communion that I know will strengthen you. The goal is for you to take just a brief amount of time each day to read and reflect, to see the circumstances in your life in the light of what you have learned in each reading, and to let God's promises of divine health fill your heart, mind, and mouth.

Each of the daily readings was selected to show you how you can personally apply and learn to eat your way to life and health. I have added several other features to help you apply and live out the truths that God wants you to know. Each daily devotional includes:

Key Verse(s): A powerful, faith-building scripture that relates to the inspirational reading, giving it a biblical foundation and anchoring your heart on the life-giving truths about the holy Communion. I encourage you to meditate on these daily scriptures. You will be surprised how much the Holy Spirit opens up God's Word to you to remind you of His love, refresh and strengthen your heart, and cause healing and life to flow into your body!

A Devotional Excerpt from *Eat Your Way to Life and Health***:** An inspiring new covenant truth that ministers God's promises of health, wholeness, and a long, abundant life. Each reading is also written to expand on a scriptural aspect of the holy Communion that will enable you to partake of the Lord's Supper with greater revelation. You will also find personal testimonies of people who applied the truths they heard me share about the Communion and experienced God's amazing healing. Where these testimonies are abridged because of space, you can find their full, personal accounts in *Eat Your Way to Life and Health.*

Today's Prayer: A faith-filled prayer meant to help you express your heart to our Lord Jesus. The prayers for each day help you to express faith in His love and His power to heal you as well as give thanks to the Father for sending us the gift of His Son. Feel free to adapt these prayers to your own situation and have heartfelt conversations with your loving Savior. May the Holy Spirit open your eyes to your rich inheritance in Christ as you commune with Him.

Today's Thought: Simple, powerful thoughts based on the daily readings and God's Word to help you focus on putting these promises of divine health into action in your life. Let these thoughts guard your mind from any fear or defeatist thought the enemy throws at you.

These ninety readings should be read at a one-each-day pace so they carry you through three months or so, giving you bite-size Bible-based teaching to build your faith as you look to the Lord for your healing or to experience greater strength and life. It is my prayer that as you journey through the powerful revelations contained in this book, you will be empowered to receive God's provision of health and wholeness through the holy Communion and walk in a greater measure of health day by day.

Our Lord is the same yesterday, today, and forever. I want to show you everlasting promises from the Word of God that He has for you. I will be sharing stories from the Bible as well as from people who have received healing even though doctors had told them their conditions were terminal or incurable. What God has done for them, He can do for you too.

If you are battling a serious illness today or your loved one is facing a health challenge, I have prepared testimonies from those who have experienced healing after receiving a revelation of Jesus' finished work and of the holy Communion. These are personal accounts additional to those already in *Eat Your Way to Life and Health*. As you read them, may your heart be encouraged, your hope renewed, and your faith strengthened to receive the healing you are believing our faithful Lord Jesus for.

My friend, your healing breakthrough is on its way, and I can't wait for you to receive every iota of the blessings our Lord Jesus paid for you to enjoy. Let me show you how you can eat your way to life and health.

SECTION I

COME TO THE TABLE

For I received from the Lord that which I also delivered to you: that the Lord Jesus on the same night in which He was betrayed took bread; and when He had given thanks, He broke it and said, "Take, eat; this is My body which is broken for you; do this in remembrance of Me."

In the same manner He also took the cup after supper, saying, "This cup is the new covenant in My blood. This do, as often as you drink it, in remembrance of Me."

For as often as you eat this bread and drink this cup, you proclaim the Lord's death till He comes.

—1 Corinthians 11:23–26

DAY 1
HEALING ALL

How God anointed Jesus of Nazareth with the Holy Spirit and with power, who went about doing good and healing all who were oppressed by the devil, for God was with Him.

—Acts 10:38

Would you agree that apart from the gift of salvation—receiving Jesus as our Lord and being saved from eternal destruction—the greatest blessing we could receive is health? You can have a wonderful family, but if you are flat on your back and cannot enjoy being with them, that would be misery. As for money, you might be able to afford the latest medical treatment or best surgeons, but all the money in the world cannot buy health.

I fully believe that our Lord Jesus, who went about healing all who were bound by sickness and disease, wants you healed, well, and full of life. And I believe He has given me a mission to teach on the health-giving, life-imparting, healing power of the holy Communion. This is not a new revelation or some passing fad. For almost two decades I have been preaching, teaching, and practicing the insights the Lord has given me. Every Sunday, at every one of our church services, including our kids' services, we partake of the holy Communion together. I am fully convinced of its efficacy, and I personally partake of the Lord's Supper on a daily basis. I can't begin to tell you how the freedom to receive the Lord's Supper has blessed my family and me.

I have preached many messages on the holy Communion, but I preached what I consider to be a milestone message on April 7, 2002, titled "Health and Wholeness Through the Holy Communion." The truths unveiled that day led to the healing and transformation of umpteen lives around the world and released a flood tide of revelations that continue to reverberate through many lives. My friend, I don't want *you* to miss out on that message! So I have prepared a link to the message as my gift to you. You can listen to it by going to JosephPrince.com/eat. I believe this is a word the Lord put in my heart *for you* many years ago. It was powerful then, but it has never been more relevant than right now.

I pray that your life will be revolutionized as the Lord reveals His truths to you. Whatever sickness or pain you might be dealing with, may your healing begin today.

TODAY'S THOUGHT

Don't ever doubt that our Lord Jesus wants you to enjoy His blessing of health. When He walked on earth, He didn't walk on water or calm storms all the time, but He *healed* all the time. Every village He stepped into, everywhere He traveled, He went about doing good and healing all who were oppressed. He will do the same for you.

TODAY'S PRAYER

Father, thank You for inviting me to come to You for a revelation of the life-imparting, healing power of the holy Communion. Open the eyes of my heart to see Jesus, who went about doing good and healing all who were in need. I believe the more I learn about His love and how I can partake of His finished work through the Communion, the more I will experience Your provision of healing. Amen.

DAY 2

PERFECTION IS NOT REQUIRED

For He made Him who knew no sin to be sin for us, that we might become the righteousness of God in Him.

—2 Corinthians 5:21

When I was a young Christian, I was a victim of a flawed, legalistic teaching based on a misinterpretation of the apostle Paul's teaching on the holy Communion in 1 Corinthians 11:27–30:

> *"Therefore whoever eats this bread or drinks this cup of the Lord in an unworthy manner will be guilty of the body and blood of the Lord. But let a man examine himself, and so let him eat of the bread and drink of the cup.* For he who eats and drinks in an unworthy manner eats and drinks judgment to himself, not discerning the Lord's body. For this reason many are weak and sick among you, and many sleep."

I was taught and warned, as perhaps you were, that if there was *any* sin in my life, including ones I didn't know about or had forgotten to confess, that sin made me *unworthy* to partake of the holy Communion. I would bring judgment and sickness on myself, and I might even die before my time! But how could I ever know if I was "worthy" enough? I was not living in sin or anything like that, but I knew that to God, sin is sin, and if anyone fails in even one area, he is counted guilty of all (James 2:10). As a result, I was so fearful of the Communion I did not partake of it for many years. After all, I was no fool. Why would I risk it?

I was robbed of my inheritance because of well-meaning but erroneous preaching that put an invisible fence around what was meant to be a *source* of health and healing and a blessing for God's people. A fence was put around it saying, "Don't come near unless you are worthy."

Don't be robbed like I was.

This is what the Word of God says: Jesus' blood has already been shed for us, and as believers, we *are* the righteousness of God in Christ (2 Cor. 5:21). We are completely righteous and worthy not because we are perfect, but because *He* is perfect. He paid the full price for the forgiveness of our sins, which alone makes us worthy. His sacrifice at the cross has fully qualified us to receive His healing *and* victory over sin and every kind of bondage that is robbing us of health and life.

TODAY'S THOUGHT

While sin is destructive and we are certainly against sin, we don't have to be perfect to come to the Lord's Table. If that were a prerequisite, *no one* would be able to partake! Thank God that even when we fail, we have "redemption through His blood, the forgiveness of sins, according to the riches of His grace" (Eph. 1:7).

TODAY'S PRAYER

Lord Jesus, thank You that in You I am the righteousness of God. Thank You that because of Your gift of righteousness to me, I stand completely forgiven, with every sin paid for. You have made me worthy to partake of the Communion, and I will come fearlessly and gladly and receive healing, life, and all that You have for me. Amen.

DAY 3
DON'T BE ROBBED

Beware lest anyone cheat you through philosophy and empty deceit, according to the tradition of men, according to the basic principles of the world, and not according to Christ.

—Colossians 2:8

In yesterday's reading, I hope you saw clearly that in 1 Corinthians 11 the apostle Paul did not say that those who are *unworthy* cannot partake of the Communion. Reread those verses closely. Paul was talking about the unworthy *manner* in which one partakes of the Communion. He was writing to the Corinthian church, whose members were treating the Lord's Supper with irreverence, eating to satisfy their hunger with no consideration for others, and even getting drunk (1 Cor. 11:20–22 AMP).

It is clear Paul was correcting them for treating the Lord's Supper like any other meal, rather than partaking of it in a *manner* that was worthy of what our Lord Jesus had ordained it to be. They were treating the Communion as something ordinary instead of seeing it as holy and set apart.

For us today, to partake of the Communion in an unworthy manner is to treat the elements of the Communion as *common*, *insignificant*, and *powerless*. It is to treat the Communion elements as natural and ordinary, as nothing more than a cracker and some juice, and to fail to recognize the potent, sacred force we get to hold in our hands. It is to disdain the elements and to be like the children of Israel, who got so familiar with the manna God in His grace provided that they saw the bread from heaven as worthless (Num. 21:5). It is to simply go through the motions of eating the bread and taking the cup without valuing the significance and power they contain.

Maybe you have never really understood why Christians partake of the Communion. Maybe it is an empty ritual to you, something you do because your church conducts it occasionally. Maybe you are partaking of the Communion because you heard healing testimonies from others, and you are hoping it might work its "magic" for you too. Or maybe you see it as a sentimental custom or quaint tradition that simply reminds Christians about the roots of their faith.

If any of those maybes describe you, may I tell you that *you* have been robbed? The good news is, God is reaching out to you through the pages of this book to bring you a clear understanding of what the holy Communion is really about. I pray that as you keep on reading over the course of these ninety days, your eyes will be opened and your body will fully receive the healing power of the holy Communion!

TODAY'S THOUGHT

The Bible says God's people are destroyed "for lack of knowledge" (Hos. 4:6). Your lack of knowledge about what the holy Communion is really about has been destroying you, and you don't even know it! It's time to take back what the enemy has stolen.

TODAY'S PRAYER

Father God, thank You for showing me that the elements of the holy Communion are not common, insignificant, and powerless but powerful to effect the healing You want me to experience. Thank You for Your Word that renews my mind to Your eternal truths about the Communion. I declare that I will not be robbed of its power. Amen.

DAY 4

THE REAL FOUNTAIN OF YOUTH

Now on the first day of the week . . . the disciples came together to break bread.

—Acts 20:7

Let me tell you why I believe the holy Communion is more powerful than any medicine, any medical procedure, any antibiotic, and any chemotherapy used to heal our bodies. Let me tell you why I believe the holy Communion is the proverbial "fountain of youth" mankind has been in search of for generations and why I believe every time we partake of it, we are causing our youth to be renewed like the eagle's (Ps. 103:5).

The earth has been under a divine judgment ever since Adam sinned. Aging, disease, and death are all part of this divine sentence. The reality is, we live in a fallen world and these effects of the divine sentence are happening to our mortal bodies. But God never intended for His children to suffer any of it. That is why He sent His Son to bear our sins and sicknesses on the cross. That is why He provided the holy Communion as a way to escape the divine judgment that is on this world, to offset its effects. The holy Communion is a supernatural channel for His health and wholeness to flow into our bodies. While the world is getting weaker and sicker, I believe we are getting stronger and healthier each time we partake of the Communion by faith!

The early church clearly understood how powerful the Communion is. That's why the Bible tells us they broke bread "from house to house" (Acts 2:46). When they met on Sunday, the main reason wasn't to hear preaching and teaching—"The disciples came together *to break bread*" (Acts 20:7). Even though the apostle Paul was the guest speaker that weekend, the main reason they gathered was to break bread.

If people today knew the magnitude of the power contained within the Lord's Supper, they would be like the early church, partaking of the Lord's Supper as often as they could and receiving as many of His benefits as they could. We have been robbed, people! It's time to wake up!

TODAY'S THOUGHT

Let us always partake in a manner *worthy* of the Lord's Supper, with a revelation of His finished work. Let us always be conscious that, as we partake of the bread, we are partaking of Jesus' body that was broken so ours might be whole (1 Cor. 11:24; Isa. 53:5). And as we partake of the cup, let us be conscious we are receiving His blood that was shed for the forgiveness and remission of *all* our sins (Matt. 26:28; Col. 2:13).

TODAY'S PRAYER

Heavenly Father, help me to be like the early church and understand how powerful the holy Communion is. Whenever I partake, help me to see the bread as Jesus' body broken for my healing and the cup as His blood shed for the forgiveness of all my sins. I release my faith to receive all its blessings and benefits. Amen.

DAY 5

A VERY PRESENT HELP

God is our refuge and strength, a very present help in trouble.

—Psalm 46:1

If God wants us to be healthy, and Jesus' body was broken for us, why are there Christians who are sick? I personally know believers who are battling severe illnesses, and I am sure you do too. You or your loved one might even be facing a health challenge right now.

If you are fighting a medical condition, please know that it is okay for you to have doubts and questions. The Lord knows the confusion and pain you feel, and He wants you to know He is with you through it all. I know it can be hard to keep trusting Him when you are going through a fiery trial. But keep trusting Him, my friend. He is, right now, your very *present* help. Keep fixing your eyes on Him. He is faithful, and He will never leave you nor forsake you (Deut. 31:6).

Daniel 3 records the story of three friends (Shadrach, Meshach, and Abed-Nego), who were bound and thrown into a fiery furnace when they refused to bow to and worship the gold image set up by King Nebuchadnezzar. The furnace was so hot that the men who threw them in were killed by the heat. But the king saw the three friends walking in the midst of the fire, and he saw a fourth man with them who was "like the Son of God" (Dan. 3:25). Amazed, the king called them out, and he and all his officials saw that the fire had had no power over them. Not a single hair on them was singed, their clothes were not scorched or damaged, and there was not even the smell of smoke on them. Why? Because the Lord was with them, protecting and delivering them. As a result, the king acknowledged that there was no other god who could deliver like their God, and the three friends were not only released, they were also promoted.

TODAY'S THOUGHT

Even if you are going through a trial, the Lord will deliver you. Just as He was in the fire with Daniel's three friends, He is *with you*. I pray in Jesus' name you will emerge from this trial so much stronger than before you went in. I declare that this disease shall have *no* power over you and that the Lord will deliver you so completely you will come out of this without even the smell of smoke on you!

TODAY'S PRAYER

Lord Jesus, there is truly no other god who saves and delivers like You. Thank You for showing me I need not fear even when I am in the blazing furnace, because You are with me and will walk with me in the fire and protect me. I believe that nothing shall by any means hurt me, and that even now, You are delivering me from the physical conditions in my body. Thank You, Lord. Amen.

DAY 6

FORGIVEN AND HEALED

Bless the Lord, O my soul,
And forget not all His benefits:
Who forgives all your iniquities,
Who heals all your diseases.

—Psalm 103:2–3

It's interesting that the apostle Paul draws our attention to the reason many Christians are weak, sick, and even dying prematurely. I am not saying every believer's sickness is due to this, but God's Word highlights it. This is good news because it means that when we know what this reason is, we can avoid it. Paul says, "For he who eats and drinks in an unworthy manner eats and drinks judgment to himself, *not discerning the Lord's body. For this reason* many are weak and sick among you, and many sleep" (1 Cor. 11:29–30).

The "reason" highlighted by Paul is "not discerning the Lord's body." The word *discerning* is translated from the Greek word *diakrino*, which means "to make a distinction."[1] There are some who recognize that Jesus' blood was shed for the forgiveness of our sins, but they don't recognize that His body was broken so that our bodies can be well. There are also those who lump both the bread and cup as one, seeing both as representing the forgiveness of sins instead of separating the two. But the same Jesus who purchased the forgiveness of all our sins also removed all our diseases. The failure to make a distinction and see that the Lord's body was broken for our diseases to be healed causes many to be sick and weak.

If many are sick and weak because they have failed to discern the Lord's body, then it stands to reason the opposite is true: those who discern that His body was broken for their health will be healthy and strong and will live good, long lives! There is such healing power in the holy Communion, but too many people have been robbed of this gift either because they do not know about it or because they have been taught wrongly about what the Lord meant for it to be. I believe that as you grow in your revelation of how His body was broken for yours to be whole, you will find yourself receiving a greater and greater measure of His healing and divine life!

TODAY'S THOUGHT

Every time we partake of the Lord's body, we are ingesting health, vitality, strength, and long life. If there is disease in the body, the disease will be supernaturally driven out. If there is decay and degeneration, the deterioration will be reversed. If there is pain, it will be removed. The results may not be spectacular and immediate, but they are sure and will surely come. And I pray you will experience them for yourself.

TODAY'S PRAYER

Lord Jesus, thank You for showing me how to rightly discern Your body as I partake of the holy Communion. Thank You for loving me so much, You allowed Your body to be broken for mine to be whole. You suffered so that I don't have to bear the symptoms and pains in my body. I believe that even now, You are driving out disease and removing all my pain. Through the Communion, I believe I am receiving more and more of Your health, vitality, strength, and long life. Amen.

DAY 7

COME BOLDLY TO THE TABLE

"With God all things are possible."

—Matthew 19:26

Some years ago, doctors discovered a huge cancerous tumor in my uncle's throat. After a more detailed scan, a pathologist told him the cancer was aggressively spreading all over his neck and behind his tongue. In that moment my uncle said he gave up hope he would live. But before his surgery to try to remove the tumor, his daughters approached him and said, "Let's have Communion together, Dad. Let's pray and believe God."

He shared that as they partook of the Communion, he felt hope rising in his heart for the first time, and he partook, believing that Jesus was his healer and believing that the body of Jesus would make a difference in his body right there in the hospital ward. After the doctors removed the tumor, amazingly the biopsy showed absolutely no trace of cancer in the tumor even though multiple scans before the surgery had confirmed it was cancerous and of an aggressive nature. Somehow the Lord had caused the cancer to supernaturally disappear, and I believe it happened when my uncle and his family partook of the Communion.

In the same way, if your doctors have given you a negative prognosis, do not fear or despair. Don't live as though you don't have a Savior. We may not know how our healing can take place, but let's have faith in the finished work of Jesus. He has paid the price for you to be well and made it easy for you to receive not just His love and forgiveness, but His healing power as well.

I pray that this section has helped to answer some of your questions about the holy Communion and that you are now excited to receive its benefits freely. I want to invite you to the Lord's Table. The table has been prepared, not by human hands that can falter and fail, but by the perfect One whose hands were nailed to the cross for you. He invites you to come to partake of His body broken for you and His blood shed for you. Come boldly to the table and partake by faith and receive your healing.

TODAY'S THOUGHT

If you have received Jesus as your Lord and Savior, you have been made worthy by the blood of the Lamb. You have been washed clean of all your sins. Don't allow the enemy to rob you any longer. Partake of the Lord's Supper with thanksgiving, knowing that each time you partake, you are getting healthier and stronger!

TODAY'S PRAYER

Father, thank You that with You on my side, all things are possible. Thank You that Your Son, the perfect One whose hands were nailed to the cross for me, has prepared the table for me. I will come boldly to the table, partake by faith, and receive my healing. Amen.

SECTION II

NOT ANOTHER DIET PLAN

"I am the living bread which came down from heaven. If anyone eats of this bread, he will live forever; and the bread that I shall give is My flesh, which I shall give for the life of the world." . . . Then Jesus said to them, "Most assuredly, I say to you, unless you eat the flesh of the Son of Man and drink His blood, you have no life in you. Whoever eats My flesh and drinks My blood has eternal life, and I will raise him up at the last day. For My flesh is food indeed, and My blood is drink indeed. He who eats My flesh and drinks My blood abides in Me, and I in him."

—John 6:51, 53–56

DAY 8

THE ANSWER IS IN REDEMPTION

For it is good that the heart be established by grace, not with foods which have not profited those who have been occupied with them.

—Hebrews 13:9

You may have picked up my book *Eat Your Way to Life and Health* thinking I am advocating a new dieting plan. The reality is, I am! But the food and drink I am talking about are not natural food and drink. In this section, I want to talk to you more about this *supernatural* food and drink and the key to living a long, healthy life *God's way.*

Many people are pursuing food and diet as their key to health. I personally observe a healthy diet, and I am all for exercise and go for walks on a regular basis. But may I tell you that eating right doesn't guarantee good health? For instance, I agree with those who advocate that the Mediterranean diet, which our Lord Jesus would have eaten, is good, but every single person Jesus healed was on that diet and still fell sick. Those who eat the best organic superfoods and are phenomenally disciplined with their exercise routine still fall terminally ill and have their lives shortened by sickness. Why is that? Creation is fallen. The answer is not found in *creation*; it is found in *redemption*!

If you have been on such diets and they have been good for you, praise the Lord! I am just saying our trust and dependence cannot be in the foods we eat to make us healthy or to give us long lives. There is no hope in a fallen creation. All of creation is groaning and subject to death and decay (Rom. 8:21–22 NLT). Hebrews 13:9 even tells us the only sure thing we should establish our hearts on is grace, not food, and grace is the very person of our Lord Jesus. The only guarantee is the finished work of our Lord Jesus Christ.

God spent just one chapter in the whole Bible talking about creation. When it comes to redemption, however, God spent more than ten chapters in Exodus alone talking about the blood sacrifices, offerings, and tabernacle of Moses because they all speak of the glories and beauties of His Son and the supernatural work of redemption He was sent to carry out.

For God to create, He only had to speak. But for God to redeem us, He had to *bleed*. If we think we can achieve the blessing of health by our discipline and good works, we are saying the cross was useless and Jesus' sufferings were in vain. But, my friend, that is not so. There is no hope in creation; there is only hope in the cross!

TODAY'S THOUGHT

Our Lord Jesus has something special set aside for His people, and that's the gift of His divine health. His way is a *supernatural* health based on the supernatural work of redemption. Even as we eat healthily and exercise regularly, if we want to walk in supernatural health, our trust should be in a supernatural God and the supernatural food He has given us through the holy Communion.

TODAY'S PRAYER

Father God, thank You that Your Word declares the supernatural work of redemption that our Lord Jesus carried out on the cross. Today I put my hope in His finished work alone. As I partake of the supernatural food You have given, I believe You are causing me to walk in Your supernatural health. All glory to Jesus! Amen.

DAY 9

GOD'S ORDAINED WAY

"I am the living bread which came down from heaven. If anyone eats of this bread, he will live forever; and the bread that I shall give is My flesh, which I shall give for the life of the world."

—John 6:51

Let me tell you more about this supernatural food and drink we get to take. It is the only food and drink that is not based on fallen creation or dependent on the efforts of fallen man. When we eat and drink this supernatural food, we are partaking of the work of redemption and not creation.

In the above verse, when the Lord Jesus said He is the living bread, the word *life* here is the Greek word *zoe*, which is the same Greek word used in the Septuagint when God breathed into Adam and Adam received life (Gen. 2:7). While *zoe* refers to the life that God lives by, *zoe* also refers to physical life, health, vitality, and wholeness.[1] The food that God has given us to eat is not perishable food but *living* bread—Jesus, who came from heaven and was given for us to have life.

There are some who think Jesus was simply talking about believing in Him. But our Lord Jesus went on to say, "For My flesh is food indeed, and My blood is drink indeed. He who *eats* My flesh and drinks My blood abides in Me, and I in him" (John 6:55–56).

Did you know two different Greek words are used here for the word *eats*? When Jesus said, "If anyone *eats* of this bread, he will live forever"

(John 6:51), the generic Greek word *phago* for *eats* was used. *Phago* can be used in a physical sense or in a spiritual sense, as in to feed on Christ.[2] But when Jesus said, "He who *eats* My flesh and drinks My blood abides in Me, and I in him" (John 6:56), the Greek word used for *eats* is *trogo*, which means "to gnaw or crunch,"[3] like when eating nuts. There is no way you can spiritualize a crunching sound. Jesus was not talking about spiritually eating or feeding here. He was talking about physically eating, about chewing with a crunching sound!

To understand more what our Lord was referring to, consider what He was talking about on the night of His betrayal when He broke the bread and gave it to His disciples, saying, "Take, eat; this is My body." And consider what He was referring to when He gave them the cup, saying, "This is My blood of the new covenant, which is shed for many for the remission of sins" (Matt. 26:26–28). Yes, He was talking about His coming crucifixion, but He was also instituting the holy Communion, a physical meal.

The Communion is God's ordained way or delivery system for us to receive the unending, holy, youthful, overcoming, and perpetually healthy life Jesus has as we "eat His flesh and drink His blood." All that is required is that you come boldly and partake, believing that His finished work qualifies you for any healing you need!

TODAY'S THOUGHT

The Bible tells us that "the whole multitude sought to touch Him, for power went out from Him and healed them all" (Luke 6:19). Our Lord Jesus' body emanated such divine health, power, and life that simply touching even the hem of His garment caused many to be healed (Mark 6:56). Can you imagine the power we are ingesting when we partake of the bread and cup—His broken body and shed blood?

TODAY'S PRAYER

Lord Jesus, I believe You are the living bread who came from heaven and gave Your life that I might have life. Thank You that You ordained the Communion as the delivery system for me to receive the unending, holy, youthful, overcoming, and perpetually healthy life that is Yours. Thank You for infusing me with divine health, power, and life as I partake of the bread and cup. Amen.

DAY 10

STRIPED, PIERCED, AND BURNT

The Lord Jesus on the same night in which He was betrayed took bread; and when He had given thanks, He broke it and said, "Take, eat; this is My body which is broken for you; do this in remembrance of Me."

—1 Corinthians 11:23–24

Why did our Lord Jesus choose the bread and wine as the elements He wanted us to partake of "in remembrance" of Him? I believe it is because they are practical and visual reminders of what happened to Him as He went to the cross. Let's first consider the bread.

The bread our Lord Jesus broke on the night of the Passover was unleavened Jewish matzah bread, which is a flat, cracker-like bread specially prepared for the Passover. I want to highlight this because today most of us think of soft, fluffy loaves when we mention bread. But this is not the kind of bread Jesus was talking about.

When our church was smaller, we purchased matzah bread and broke it into pieces for our congregation when we partook of the holy Communion together each week. As we ate the bread, we could hear crunching sounds from the people around us, and I believe we were hearing the scripture in John 6:56 being fulfilled—hearing what it sounds like to *trogo* or "to crunch"!

Jewish leaders who didn't even believe in Jesus have passed down through the centuries the instructions for making the matzah bread. If you look at the picture of the matzah bread on the next page, you will notice it is striped, pierced, and burnt.

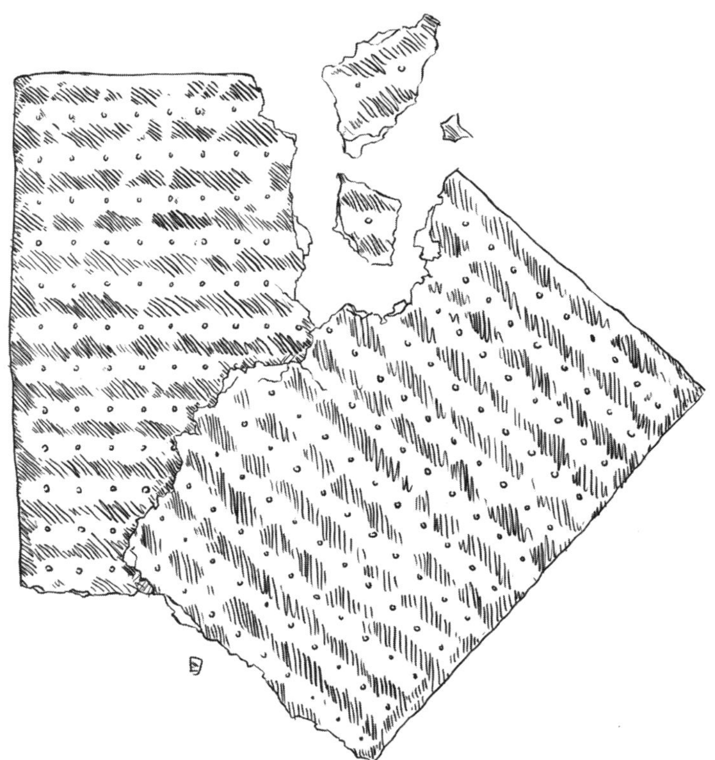

The matzah bread is a practical, visual reminder of what Jesus suffered for our healing.

Do you know why the matzah bread is made this way? I believe the Lord ordained it to be striped, pierced, and burnt so that each time you partake of the holy Communion, you are reminded afresh what Jesus went through for you:

- *Striped*—because it is by the stripes He bore when the soldiers scourged Him that we are healed (Isa. 53:5).
- *Pierced*—because His hands and feet were pierced by the nails, His side was pierced by the soldier's spear (John 19:34), and His brow was pierced by the crown of thorns (John 19:2).
- *Burnt*—because the fire of God's judgment fell upon Him when He carried our sins (Isa. 53:4).

Receiving the Communion is really about releasing your faith to see His body broken and striped for your healing and wholeness as you partake of the bread. It's about receiving His love, knowing He suffered for you so that you could receive the healing He wants you to have.

TODAY'S THOUGHT

Because Jesus' body was striped, pierced, and burnt on the cross, we can have full assurance sickness and disease have *no right* to be in our bodies. Our Lord Jesus has already borne every sickness on His body and reversed every curse by His death. Today we can receive all that Jesus did on the cross by partaking of the holy Communion—through the simple act of eating.

TODAY'S PRAYER

Father in heaven, thank You for this powerful, visual reminder that our Lord Jesus was striped, pierced, and burnt for our healing. Thank You that I can receive all that Jesus did for me on the cross through the simple act of eating as I receive the holy Communion in faith. I declare that sickness and disease have no right to be in my body. In Jesus' name, amen.

DAY 11

WHAT THE SAVIOR ENDURED

His visage was marred more than any man,
And His form more than the sons of men.

—Isaiah 52:14

Our Lord Jesus chose the bread and wine as the elements of the holy Communion because they are practical, visual reminders of what happened to Him as He went to the cross. Both grain and grapes have to go through a process of being pulverized before you can get bread or wine.

You don't get wine from just eating grapes. The grapes have to first be trampled upon and completely crushed. They are then left in the dark to ferment. That's what happened to our Lord Jesus.

It is important we discern the Lord's body for our health. Each time you partake of His broken body by eating the bread, don't rush through it. Partake with a revelation of what He did for you, and meditate on the process the bread had to go through. To get bread in Jesus' time, the wheat stalks first had to be threshed, either through beating (Judg. 6:11 NASB) or with the use of a threshing sledge (Isa. 41:15). It was a violent process that involved beating, crushing, and cutting the wheat to separate the grain from the stalks. Then the grain had to be ground in a millstone or beaten in a mortar to get flour. After that, water had to be added, and the flour was then kneaded and punched into dough before it was baked over fire.

All this is a picture of what happened to our Lord Jesus. To become the Bread of Life for you and me, He was brutally beaten and pounded over and over again during His trial and crucifixion. When He was condemned by the high priest and Sanhedrin, they mocked Him, spat on Him, and beat Him. They blindfolded Him and struck Him on His face (Luke 22:63–64; Mark 14:65). He was then sent to Pontius Pilate, who had Him savagely scourged by Roman soldiers (Matt. 27:26). Then they put a scarlet robe on His battered body, twisted a crown of thorns, and rammed it on His head. They put a staff in His right hand, bowed before Him, and mocked Him. They spat on Him and took the staff and struck Him on the head again and again, driving the thorns deeper and deeper into His flesh with each blow. When "they were finally tired of mocking him," they led Him away to be crucified (Matt. 27:27–31 NLT).

All of that was before His body was nailed to the cross. We can never fully imagine or understand the horrifying torture, degrading humiliation, and excruciating pain our Savior endured for our sakes. He suffered so that you and I would not have to suffer the scourge of sickness in our bodies. By the scourging He bore, we are healed! Hallelujah!

TODAY'S THOUGHT

Did you know our Lord Jesus had the power to stop His ordeal and overcome His tormentors at any point? When the troops came to arrest Him, they said, "We seek Jesus of Nazareth." The Bible tells us He stepped forward and spoke the awesome name of God that was revealed to Moses—I AM (Ex. 3:14)—and the soldiers drew back and fell to the ground (John 18:5–6). That's power. But He *chose* to lay down His life and endure all the pain—for your healing and my healing. That's love!

TODAY'S PRAYER

Beloved Lord Jesus, thank You for enduring the unimaginable torture, humiliation, and pain of Your trial and the cross for me. Thank You for loving me so much that You chose to suffer and lay down Your life for me. Whenever I partake of the Communion, help me to discern Your body and have a fresh revelation of what You did to secure my healing and health. Amen.

DAY 12

BY HIS STRIPES

[Christ] Himself bore our sins in His own body on the tree, that we, having died to sins, might live for righteousness—by whose stripes you were healed.

—1 Peter 2:24

In His redemptive work, our Savior didn't want you to be saved from just your sins. If that was all He wanted to accomplish, the shedding of His perfect, atoning blood alone would have been enough. In the Old Testament, when the children of Israel brought their sacrificial animals to the priests as atonement for their sins, the animals never suffered. They were killed humanely using a method known today as *shechita* to ensure they died swiftly and painlessly.[1]

But our Lord Jesus didn't die a quick, painless death. He suffered like no other, going through hour after hour of unimaginable torture before He finally died. T. J. McCrossan, a Greek scholar, highlighted that in the original Greek text, 1 Peter 2:24 actually says, "by whose stripe you were healed." He explained that the word *stripe* was in the singular and not plural form, because Jesus was scourged till there was not even one sliver of skin left on His back. His back was one bloody stripe, one big gaping laceration.[2] According to some accounts, scourging could be so brutal that even the internal organs of the victims could be seen.[3]

The Bible tells us that our Lord Jesus was so badly mutilated He did not even look like a man anymore (Isa. 52:14). I believe the people who were present had to look away and hide their faces because they could not bear to look at His grotesque, quivering form (Isa. 53:3).

My friend, He loves you so much. He went through all that torture because a punishment was required for your well-being and health, and He allowed the punishment to fall upon Himself (Isa. 53:5 AMP). He endured it all. The unimaginable pain, the utter degradation. And the Bible tells us why: it was "for the joy that was set before Him" (Heb. 12:2).

The joy? What was the joy set before Him that gave Him such strength to endure the cross? It was His love for you! It was the joy of seeing you well, of seeing you set free from pancreatic cancer, set free from leukemia, set free from rheumatoid arthritis, set free from Lou Gehrig's disease. Whatever condition you or your loved one might have, Jesus has taken it all. He wants you to know how precious you are to Him and how loved you are today.

TODAY'S THOUGHT

Just by knowing what Jesus did for you, I believe healing has begun in your body. Whatever disease you might have been diagnosed with, Jesus bore it on His own body so you would not have to suffer it. If you are sick right now, and maybe you are reading this from your hospital bed, say this: "Thank You, Lord Jesus, You went through all that *for me*."

TODAY'S PRAYER

Lord Jesus, thank You that You are showing me Your heart of love unveiled through the unimaginable suffering and death You endured for my sake. Thank You for enduring the full punishment of the cross, for going through all that pain and suffering for the joy of securing my well-being and health. I believe and declare that by the stripes You bore, I am healed. Amen.

DAY 13

POWER TO UTTERLY DESTROY DISEASES

God has chosen the weak things of the world to put to shame the things which are mighty . . . that no flesh should glory in His presence.

—1 Corinthians 1:27, 29

For many people, it is the very simplicity of the holy Communion that makes it so hard for them to believe it can be effective. All they can see is a small piece of bread and a little cup of juice. They cannot imagine how something so seemingly insignificant, small, and weak can drive out disease or cause them to live a long life.

When we dismiss the Communion elements for those reasons, we are forgetting the way God works. The Bible says God chooses the weak things of the world to put to shame the strong. Time and again, we see how God defeated the enemies of the children of Israel not through military might but through seemingly insignificant things.

God used a sling and a stone in the hand of a young shepherd boy to bring down Goliath, the mighty champion of the Philistine army (1 Sam. 17:38–51). He used a hammer and a tent peg in the hands of a defenseless woman to destroy Sisera, the ruthless Canaanite military commander who had oppressed the children of Israel for twenty years (Judg. 4:3–22). He used the jawbone of a donkey in the hand of Samson—one man—to slay a thousand Philistines (Judg. 15:15–16).

It's interesting that when a Gentile woman came to the Lord Jesus seeking healing for her severely demonized daughter, He referred to healing as "the children's bread." Do you know what the woman said to Him? "Yes, Lord, yet even the little dogs eat the crumbs which fall from their masters' table." Jesus then said to her, "O woman, great is your faith! Let it be to you as you desire." And that very hour, her daughter was healed (Matt. 15:22–28).

What do you think the children's bread that is laid on the "masters' table" is a shadow of? The holy Communion! You and I sit at the Master's table because we are sons and daughters of the Most High God, and we partake freely of the Lord's Supper. If the seemingly insignificant "crumbs" that fell from the table could heal the woman's child, how much more healing and life we shall receive when we have the substance of the holy Communion!

TODAY'S THOUGHT

When you hold the elements of the Communion in your hands, they may appear small and inconsequential. Your flesh may try to tell you, "This is silly. What can this little cracker do?" or "There's no point getting your hopes up. Nothing can help you." But don't listen to those lies. Don't make the mistake of despising the bread and the cup, because God can use what seems so small to utterly destroy diseases the world has no cure for.

TODAY'S PRAYER

Father, thank You that I can come to You, the Most High God, as Your child and sit at Your table and partake freely of the Lord's Supper. Thank You for the way You take the weak things of the world to bring to nothing the things that are mighty. I believe that as I partake of the small and seemingly insignificant elements of the Communion today, I am releasing Your mighty power to utterly destroy every evil condition in my body. Amen.

DAY 14

OUR ONLY SURETY

Then they cried out to the LORD in their trouble,
And He saved them out of their distresses.
He brought them out of darkness and the shadow
of death,
And broke their chains in pieces.

—Psalm 107:13–14

Since we are talking about how we can eat our way to life and health, I want to share a testimony from Zach, someone in Singapore who exercises almost daily and who in his own words is "careful with his diet":

> *While getting ready for work one day, I suddenly lost strength in my left leg and slid to the floor. I shouted for my wife and told her I felt unwell. I started to pray in the Spirit, calling out to Jesus. My wife also prayed and declared that by Jesus' stripes, I am healed!*
>
> *About five minutes later, strength came back to both my leg and arm, and I could stand up, but my motor skills had not returned. My family took me to the hospital where an MRI scan showed I'd suffered a mild stroke. My world sank totally. I found myself questioning,* How can this be? I exercise almost daily and I'm careful with my diet.
>
> *I was admitted to the hospital and above the door of my room hung a cross. I looked to the cross and claimed the finished work of*

Christ, pronounced my body healthy because of His perfect work, and kept claiming the finished work of Christ. We also partook of the holy Communion as a family, and I anointed myself with oil. I prayed and claimed God's promises in Psalm 23:4–6.

Over the next three days, the doctor's examinations confirmed that my strength had returned to around 80 to 85 percent and finally to 95 percent, and I was discharged. In my follow-up review, I was given the all clear to go back to my regular exercise routine. Soon after that, I competed in an 18K run and finished it in just over two hours.

I give Jesus all the praise! Amen.

A stroke can lead to permanent damage in the body. I fully believe that Zach's speedy recovery was because of the Lord's protection and healing. But what I want you to see is this: Zach was perplexed that he could suffer a stroke since he exercised almost daily and was careful with his diet. At the end of the day, Zach's dependence could not be on his eating and exercising. He could only look to the cross and depend on the finished work of Christ. And that's our only surety as well. As you look to your Savior and see His perfect work availing for you today, you will also see Him rescue you from all your distresses!

TODAY'S THOUGHT

If you find yourself facing a medical condition, may I encourage you to do what Zach did? No matter how dire your prognosis continues to be, declare that your body is healthy because of Jesus' perfect work, and keep standing on His finished work. Keep speaking His Word over yourself and keep thanking the Lord for His promises.

TODAY'S PRAYER

Father, there is no other god like You. Thank You that nothing is too hard for You, and because of Jesus' perfect work, there is no disease or condition that is too advanced for Your deliverance and complete healing. Even as I see symptoms in my body, I choose to speak Your Word and promises. And as I partake of the Communion today, I see myself healed and well because of what Jesus has done for me. Amen.

DAY 15

DO NOT FEAR

Yea, though I walk through the valley of the
shadow of death,
I will fear no evil;
For You are with me;
Your rod and Your staff, they comfort me.
You prepare a table before me in the presence of
my enemies;
You anoint my head with oil;
My cup runs over.
Surely goodness and mercy shall follow me
All the days of my life.

—Psalm 23:4–6

In yesterday's testimony, Zach had the terrifying experience of suddenly losing strength in half of his body, but he kept speaking the promises of Psalm 23:4–6 over himself. Do as Zach did and know that even if you are walking through a dark valley and the shadow of death looms over you, you do not have to fear, for the Lord is *with you.*

Notice that the Lord prepares a table before you *in the presence* (not in the absence) of your enemies. The apostle Paul referred to the holy Communion as "the Lord's table" (1 Cor. 10:21). That means even when the symptoms are in your body, and even when the pain is there, the Lord wants you to come to His table and eat. By partaking of the holy Communion, eat and receive of all that our Lord Jesus has done for you on the cross. His body was broken so that yours might be whole.

It is human nature to feast and celebrate only *after* we see that our problems have been solved and our enemies eradicated. But that's not what God wants you to do. He loves you so much, and right now He says to you, "Rest. Sit down. Eat. For I will fight your battle. I will defeat your enemies!" As you eat at His table, see yourself getting supernaturally stronger. See the tumor shriveling up. See His health flowing into your body.

Don't be afraid of your enemies. They might be all around you, but you can eat from the Lord's Table with joy, knowing that *surely*, goodness and mercy and His unfailing love *follow* after you all the days of your life! If you look up the Hebrew word for *follow* in Psalm 23:6, you will see that it is *radaph*, which means "to chase, hunt, or pursue."[1] See your Daddy God's goodness and love chasing you down wherever you go. Even if you have to undergo surgery, chemotherapy, or an organ transplant, He is right there with you. In the operating theater, He is there. In the intensive care unit, He is there. Do not fear—He is with you, and your enemies have *no power* over you!

TODAY'S THOUGHT

If your doctor has prescribed medicines for you, please continue to take them together with the holy Communion. But even as you take them or undergo treatment, your trust can be in your Lord Jesus to heal you. Medicines are man-made and come with warnings listing all their possible side effects. But the holy Communion was provided by God Himself, and the only side effects are that you will get younger and stronger each time you partake of it!

TODAY'S PRAYER

Lord Jesus, I thank You that You have prepared the table in the presence of my enemies, even as I feel the symptoms and pain in my body. I gladly come to the table and receive Your goodness and the healing I need. Thank You that Your goodness and love are chasing me down wherever I go, even into treatment and surgery. By faith I see Your health flowing into my body, and I will not be afraid. Amen.

SECTION III

NONE FEEBLE, NONE SICK

Then Moses called for all the elders of Israel and said to them, "Pick out and take lambs for yourselves according to your families, and kill the Passover lamb. And you shall take a bunch of hyssop, dip it in the blood that is in the basin, and strike the lintel and the two doorposts with the blood that is in the basin. And none of you shall go out of the door of his house until morning. For the LORD will pass through to strike the Egyptians; and when He sees the blood on the lintel and on the two doorposts, the LORD will pass over the door and not allow the destroyer to come into your houses to strike you."

—Exodus 12:21–23

DAY 16

"WHY IS THIS NIGHT DIFFERENT?"

"It shall be, when your children say to you, 'What do you mean by this service?' that you shall say, 'It is the Passover sacrifice of the Lord, who passed over the houses of the children of Israel in Egypt when He struck the Egyptians and delivered our households.'"

—Exodus 12:26–27

I believe that in this section, as you begin to see the beautiful and powerful truths from the Passover meal the children of Israel ate in Egypt, your faith to receive all the Lord has for you will be enlarged. And as your revelation grows, faith will follow. Faith is not a struggle. The more you see Jesus and all He has done for you, the more you will have faith to receive your healing. You may be amazed to discover that the Passover meal foreshadowed our eating of the holy Communion today—and they both point to the finished work at the cross!

Years ago I was in Israel and had the privilege of celebrating the Jewish Passover with a family of Messianic believers who were completely transformed by the gospel of grace. During that Passover meal, what stood out distinctively to me was the question the children at the table asked the elders: "Why is this night different from all other nights?" While they were following an oral tradition of the Jewish people, this question set up the opportunity for the elders to share with the next generation how the Lord had delivered the children of Israel from slavery and bondage (Ex. 7—11). As the elders retold the story, the children heard how the blood of a lamb without blemish protected the Israelites from the angel of death that struck dead every firstborn son in Egypt and caused Pharaoh to finally let the Israelites go.

Can you see how even back then, God was already looking forward in time to His Son's death and how He would shed His blood to deliver you and me from the darkness and slavery of sin and sickness?

When you partake of the holy Communion, I want you to ask yourself the same question the children asked: "Why is this night different?" It might not be nighttime when you are partaking of the holy Communion, but as you partake like this, you are remembering what happened when our Lord Jesus was nailed to the cross, suspended between heaven and earth, and rejected by man and by God. When Jesus was born, midnight became midday as angels filled the sky and the glory of God shone all around (Luke 2:8–11). But as Jesus hung on the cross for you and me, midday became midnight as darkness covered the land (Matt. 27:45).

My friend, if you are going through a dark period, take heart. Your Savior went through the darkness so you can always stand in His wonderful light (1 Peter 2:9) and see the Sun of Righteousness arise with healing in His wings (Mal. 4:2).

TODAY'S THOUGHT

Because of what happened that day on the cross, you can trust God for freedom from the disease that has shackled you. You can freely receive the blessings of abundant life, health, and strength. You can rest in the knowledge that you have been marked and covered by the blood of His protection and no plague can come near your dwelling. You can have the confidence that the same God who freed a whole nation from oppression fights for you.

And if God is for you, no sickness, no virus, and no medical condition can prevail against you (Rom. 8:31)!

TODAY'S PRAYER

Father, thank You for reminding me how Jesus went through terrible darkness at the cross so that I can always stand in the light of His healing and protection. I declare that I am covered by His blood today. Because of His blood You are for me today, and therefore no sickness, no virus, and no medical condition can prevail against me. Hallelujah! Thank You, Father. Amen.

DAY 17

SHADOW VERSUS SUBSTANCE

"Your lamb shall be without blemish, a male of the first year. . . . And they shall take some of the blood and put it on the two doorposts and on the lintel of the houses where they eat it."

—Exodus 12:5, 7

During the Passover meal I celebrated with the Messianic family in Israel, the elders told the children about how the Lord had instructed the Israelites to select a lamb without blemish for each household. The *body* of the lamb was to be roasted and eaten with unleavened bread and bitter herbs, while its *blood* was to be applied on the lintel and two doorposts of their houses (Ex. 12:22). Can you see in the picture on the following page how applying the blood as instructed would have formed a picture of the cross?

Applying the lamb's blood on the lintel and two doorposts (top illustration) would have formed a picture of the cross (bottom illustration).

The elders narrated how the angel of death went throughout Egypt at midnight, and the cries from their Egyptian oppressors were heard throughout the land as every firstborn son—even the mighty Pharaoh's—was struck dead.

The children heard how, while this happened, their ancestors huddled together in their homes. Some were excited and expectant, knowing this was the night they would finally be freed from years of crushing slavery, while others were terrified the destroyer would also strike their homes.

But whatever their state of mind was, death *passed over* their houses as long as the blood of the lamb was on their doorposts and lintels. On that same night, Pharaoh finally let go of his stubborn grip on the children of Israel, and they began their exodus from the land of Egypt. They were free.

Every year, Jews around the world continue to reenact how the Lord rescued them so powerfully during the night of the first Passover by partaking of a carefully prepared meal and observing certain traditions. But you know what? The Passover was only a *picture* of what our Lord Jesus was going to accomplish at the cross when He delivered mankind from slavery to a greater pharaoh—Satan himself! Today we have the true Lamb of God, who has already shed His blood for us. We can confidently expect His deliverance from any bondage and oppression the enemy attempts to put us under, including sickness and disease!

TODAY'S THOUGHT

What the children of Israel had was just the shadow. What we have under the new covenant inaugurated by His shed blood is the *substance*. It was not by coincidence our Lord Jesus instituted the holy Communion on the same night He celebrated the Passover (Matt. 26:17–29; Mark 14:12–25; Luke 22:7–20). The apostle Paul referred to Him as "Christ, our Passover Lamb" (1 Cor. 5:7 NLT) because His sacrifice on the cross was the fulfillment and fullness of the Passover the children of Israel had been celebrating for generations.

TODAY'S PRAYER

Lord Jesus, thank You for showing me that the shed blood and body of the lamb without blemish in the Passover meal is but a shadow of what You accomplished at the cross to deliver me from slavery to sin and Satan himself. Thank You for becoming the true Lamb of God for me and setting me free from all sin, bondage, and sickness. Amen.

DAY 18
NONE FEEBLE

He also brought them out with silver and gold,
And there was none feeble among His tribes.

—Psalm 105:37

Do you know what happened when the children of Israel ate the Passover lamb? That very night, God liberated the Israelites from severe oppression and freed them from their captivity. But that wasn't all. The Bible also says there was *none feeble* among the six hundred thousand men who left Egypt on the night of the exodus (Ex. 12:37). But when you include the women and children, scholars estimate about two to three million Israelites were freed that night.[1]

Out of these, none—not a single one—came out feeble! Think about the backbreaking work the Israelites were forced to do and the beatings and whippings they suffered under their slave masters (Ex. 1:13–14 AMP), not to mention malnutrition from the poor diet they probably had to scrape together and the abject living conditions they must have faced. Despite years of harsh and severe labor they had to endure, there was not one who came out sick, not one who stumbled, not one who lacked strength or had mobility problems.

Do you think that in the natural, every single one in this nation of slaves could have been completely strong and healthy? Of course not. And among so many of them, I am sure there would have been elderly slaves as well. So how is it possible the Bible records that "none were feeble"?

I submit to you that something happened to their bodies on the night of the Passover as they ate the roasted lamb. I believe many among them *were* weak and sickly before the night of the Passover. But *something happened* that reversed all the effects of repetitive stress injuries, muscle and ligament strains, incapacitating work injuries, age-related conditions, and infectious diseases that could have plagued the Israelites because of the conditions they lived under. *Something happened* that night that caused them to supernaturally become healthy. The children of Israel were filled with divine strength for the journey ahead that God knew would be long, and I believe their youth was renewed like the eagle's (Ps. 103:5; Isa. 40:31).

If that could happen for the children of Israel when all they had was a natural lamb (the shadow of the true Lamb of God that you and I have), *how much more* should we see our bodies healed, our strength rejuvenated, and every weakness reversed when we partake of the holy Communion? We have the *true* Lamb of God, the *substance* and the *reality* of the shadow the Israelites believed in. *How much more* should we have none feeble and none sick among us!

TODAY'S THOUGHT

Did you know you don't have to be sick to enjoy the benefits of the Communion? Even if there is nothing wrong with you, you can believe for a greater measure of health. Whether you are partaking of the Communion for healing in your body or you are simply believing for new strength, I want you to see that you can believe for the supernatural health the Lord gave the children of Israel who partook of the Passover lamb. Those who were sick came out healed. Those who were weak came out strong. And those who were strong came out even stronger!

TODAY'S PRAYER

Father in heaven, thank You that You are a miracle-working God who fills us with divine strength for whatever journey lies ahead of us. Thank You for the true Lamb of God who heals, strengthens, and reverses weaknesses as I partake of the holy Communion. I declare that health, healing, long life, and wholeness are mine and that my youth is being renewed like the eagle's. As I partake, You are working in my body to make me stronger and healthier day by day. Amen.

DAY 19

CHRIST, OUR PASSOVER LAMB

Christ, our Passover Lamb, has been sacrificed for us.

—1 Corinthians 5:7 NLT

You may not have physical chains binding you today nor whips from brutal slave masters driving you as the Israelites did before the Passover and exodus. But maybe you are no stranger to a chronic condition that has bound you for years. Perhaps you have been tormented by recurring symptoms that have left you in constant pain. As you partake of the holy Communion, see yourself partaking of Jesus, the true Passover Lamb. Even if you don't see immediate results, keep partaking. As you partake, know your freedom is at hand. As you partake, know that you are getting stronger and healthier.

Dalene, a lady from Pennsylvania, experienced the healing power of the true Lamb of God as she partook of the holy Communion. I pray that you will be encouraged as you read her testimony:

> *On Wednesday at work, my back became very painful and I felt nauseous. I went home and slept the rest of the afternoon and through the night until late next morning. I awoke and my back was still painful so I watched your video on the holy Communion. My faith was built up to believe the oppression and pain were already borne in the body of Jesus.*

As I partook of the Communion, I saw Jesus giving me the bread, telling me, "This is My body." I ate and visualized the transformation in my body as I received His healing. I reflected that if a roasted lamb could strengthen and energize Israel, how much more would the Lamb of God heal a daughter of God. My back was immediately healed, the oppression lifted, and I was restored. Glory to God!

The grace message has transformed my life in virtually every area. Thank you so much for preaching His message.

By the way, may I draw your attention to how Dalene was watching a video that taught about the holy Communion *before* she herself partook? If you are trusting God for healing, I encourage you to do what Dalene did, to listen to teaching on the holy Communion before you partake. As you listen or watch, may your faith be built up to receive *all* the Lord has done for you, and may you also experience healing and freedom from oppression.

TODAY'S THOUGHT

If the blood of an animal could protect the children of Israel from the plague, *how much more* will the holy, sinless blood of the Son of God protect you from destruction and shield you from any sickness? I am not saying that as a believer you will never fall sick. Unfortunately, we live in a fallen world. But if you do fall sick, you have the blood-bought right to declare that by the stripes your Savior bore, you are healed. You have the blood-bought right to claim health and wholeness as your portion.

TODAY'S PRAYER

Lord Jesus, my true Passover Lamb, thank You for Your holy, sinless blood that protects me from destruction and is a shield from any sickness. As I partake of the holy Communion and eat of Your broken body, I believe I'm receiving divine health and wholeness that are my portion as God's child. I declare my blood-bought right to receive the healing You have purchased for me. Amen.

DAY 20

THE POWER OF THE BLOOD

"And when I see the blood, I will pass over you; and the plague shall not be on you to destroy you when I strike the land of Egypt."

—Exodus 12:13

Did you notice that before the Passover, God promised that when He saw the lambs' blood on the Israelites' doorposts, they would be saved from destruction? When the angel of death passed through the land, anyone among the children of Israel who was quaking in fear did so needlessly. They were saved not because they were Israelites and not because of their good behavior or anything they did. They were saved just because of one thing—the blood of the lamb.

You might be feeling anxious because doctors have detected some abnormalities in your recent health check. Or perhaps a few of your relatives have succumbed to a particular disease and you are fearful you might be next. My friend, I want you to know *you do not have to be afraid*, for *you* have been saved by the shed blood of the true Lamb of God, who takes away the sin of the world (John 1:29). If you are a believer, you can put your trust and confidence in the royal blood that flows through Immanuel's veins that is on the doorposts of your life. The cross transcends time, and on that day His blood washed you clean of *every* sin—past, present, and future. You are completely forgiven not because of your good deeds but because of His blood (Eph. 1:7). Rest in the Lamb who died for you at Calvary!

Stop disqualifying yourself from His healing because of the failures in your life. Stop believing the enemy's lies that you don't deserve to be healed because of the mistakes you have made or because you have not been going to church enough. When God looks at you, He doesn't see you in your failures and frailties. He only sees His Son because you are in Christ. Because you are *in Christ*, you are completely accepted in the Beloved (Eph. 1:6), and you are *already* blessed with every spiritual blessing (Eph. 1:3). This means that even if there are symptoms in your body, God sees you as healed. Each time you partake of the holy Communion, start seeing yourself the way God sees you. See yourself healed, whole, and filled with divine strength and life.

Each time you take up the cup of the new covenant in His blood (1 Cor. 11:25), know that the blood of Jesus "speaks better things" under the new covenant than the blood of Abel (Heb. 12:24). Abel's blood had cried out for vengeance (Gen. 4:10). Jesus' blood cries out for your redemption (Eph. 1:7; 1 Peter 1:18–19), your justification (Rom. 5:9), your victory over the enemy (Rev. 12:11), and so much more!

TODAY'S THOUGHT

Because of Jesus' blood, God imputed righteousness to you the moment you accepted Jesus as your Lord and Savior. There is no barrier between you and God (Eph. 2:13). You can come boldly before God. You can draw near to Him to find help in your time of need (Heb. 4:16; 10:19–22). Whatever challenges you might be facing, whether it is your health, emotions, finances, or relationships, you don't have to handle them alone. The Creator of all heaven and earth calls you His own precious child (John 1:12; 1 John 3:1). Run to Him!

TODAY'S PRAYER

Father God, thank You that You see the shed blood of the Lamb of God that is on the doorposts of my life. Thank You that I am completely accepted and made righteous in Your beloved Son. Because of this, I can always run to You in my time of need. Today, as I partake of the holy Communion, I declare that I am as You see me—healed, whole, and filled with divine strength and life. Amen.

DAY 21

HOW YOU EAT MATTERS

"Then they shall eat the flesh on that night; roasted in fire, with unleavened bread and with bitter herbs they shall eat it. Do not eat it raw, nor boiled at all with water, but roasted in fire—its head with its legs and its entrails."

—Exodus 12:8–9

Don't just skim through the book of Exodus and see it only as an ancient historical record. I love the little details the Holy Spirit recorded, and I believe when you take time to search out the Scriptures, the eyes of your understanding will be opened and you will see revelations of Jesus you had never seen before and experience healing and deliverance. I love seeing Jesus in the Passover.

For instance, look at God's instructions in the verses above on *how* the Israelites were to eat the Passover lamb. They were told *not* to eat the Passover lamb *raw*. How does this apply to us? When we partake of the holy Communion, we should not be focusing on our Lord Jesus' life in raw form before He had been "burned" by the fire of God's judgment on the cross. We should not be seeing Him as a baby in a manger or as He is recorded in the Gospels *before* the cross. Yes, He is a great teacher and leader. Yes, He is God incarnate. He is Immanuel, God with us. And yes, He lived a perfect life, but it wasn't His perfect life that saved us. It was His sacrifice and death on the cross. In other words, we need to see Him "roasted in fire." That's what we need to meditate on when we partake of the Communion.

The children of Israel were also told *not* to eat the lamb "boiled at all with water." I believe this means we should not water down or sanitize what Jesus did for us at the cross. As we saw previously, because of the scourging and beatings He endured, Jesus' visage, or face, was beyond recognition at the cross. His form was marred more than that of any man (Isa. 52:14). Whenever you partake of the holy Communion, picture Jesus on the cross and remember how He suffered for your forgiveness and healing.

God also told the children of Israel to eat the lamb "roasted in fire." That's a picture of God unleashing the fire of His judgment on Christ. Sin had to be punished, and as Jesus hung on the cross, He cried, "I thirst!" (John 19:28) because the fire of God's holy vengeance and righteous indignation against our sins fell upon Him. He came under the judgment of God so you and I will never come under God's judgment (Rom. 5:9–11 NLT). Because our sins have been punished in the body of our substitute, it would be unrighteous for God to punish the same sins twice.

Today God's holiness and God's righteousness are on our side, demanding our justification, demanding our forgiveness, demanding our healing, and demanding our deliverance. The next time you partake of the Communion and hold the bread in your hand, see His body burnt and smitten with your sins and diseases on the cross, and begin to walk in the full benefits of all He accomplished for you at the cross.

TODAY'S THOUGHT

On the cross, Jesus did not just take our sins; He *became* sin so we might become the righteousness of God in Him (2 Cor. 5:21). He also took our infirmities and bore our sicknesses on His own body (Isa. 53:4 YLT; Matt. 8:17). Every tumor, every cancerous growth, every deformity, every rheumatoid arthritis, every kind of disease, He took upon Himself at the cross. He bore them all so that you need not bear a single one of them in your body.

TODAY'S PRAYER

Father, thank You that the fire of Your righteous judgment for my sin was unleashed on Jesus. Thank You that I am made righteous in Him and that Your holiness and righteousness are on my side today, demanding my justification, forgiveness, and healing. Help me to see Jesus' body burnt and smitten with my sin and diseases on the cross. I receive a fresh impartation of Your love and Your healing power right now. In Jesus' name, amen.

DAY 22

JUST A GROAN WILL REACH THE THRONE

Then the children of Israel groaned because of the bondage, and they cried out; and their cry came up to God because of the bondage. So God heard their groaning, and God remembered His covenant with Abraham, with Isaac, and with Jacob.

—Exodus 2:23–24

There is an enemy who wants to keep you enslaved to that medical condition in your life. The enemy wants to keep you in a place of despair and to keep you so focused on your disappointments you cannot lay hold of God's promises for you. That is what he did to the children of Israel. When Moses told the Israelites that God would rescue them from their bondage, the Bible tells us "they refused to listen" as they had "become too discouraged by the brutality of their slavery" (Ex. 6:6–9 NLT).

But God did not abandon them even though they refused to listen. He knew they were in a state of despair because they had suffered under the yoke of slavery for so long. Do you want to know what the children of Israel did that caused God to rescue them so mightily? Read this for yourself in the verse above. The children of Israel were so oppressed all they could do was groan. There was nothing left in them to compose any prayers. And the Bible tells us *God heard their groaning* and He remembered His covenant with Abraham, Isaac, and Jacob.

I am sharing this with you because I want you to know that you *do not* need to craft impressive declarations of faith or do anything for God before He hears you. Just a groan will reach the throne. A simple sigh from you will reach the throne room of your Abba in heaven. If just a groan from the children of Israel could activate the covenant God had cut with their forefathers, *how much more* would your cry accomplish, oh child of the Most High!

If you are in a place of discouragement about your medical condition, cry out to Him and take this additional insight from the Passover as an encouragement. I love it that God told the children of Israel to partake of the Passover lamb in this manner: "And thus you shall eat it: with a belt on your waist, your sandals on your feet, and your staff in your hand" (Ex. 12:11). Why did they have to eat with belts on their waists, sandals on their feet, and staffs in their hands? God was telling them to be ready for their physical deliverance even as they ate the roasted lamb.

In the same way, when we partake of the Lord's Supper, let's partake with faith and expectancy. Our compassionate Lord Jesus has heard our groans and He is both willing and able to deliver us from any oppression. Let's partake expecting our miracle to take place, expecting our deliverance. That's what the Israelites did despite their suffering, and they came out with not one sick, not one feeble. I want to see that happening for my church and for you. We may not yet have come to the place where we can say there are "none feeble," but I believe we are on our way.

TODAY'S THOUGHT

Even if you have a medical condition or pain in your body, partake of the Lord's Supper by faith, giving thanks that you are already healed, expecting to see the full manifestation of your healing. I believe each time we partake of the Lord's Supper, we are getting healthier and healthier, stronger and stronger!

TODAY'S PRAYER

Abba, Father, thank You that You hear my every groan, that every sigh reaches Your throne, and that as I cry out to You, deliverance and healing are on the way. Thank You that as I partake of the Lord's Supper, I can partake with faith and expectancy that my miracle will take place. I give You thanks that I am already healed. In Jesus' name, amen.

DAY 23
A NEW BEGINNING

"This month shall be your beginning of months; it shall be the first month of the year to you."

—Exodus 12:2

Perhaps you are thinking to yourself, *I tried partaking of the holy Communion before but it didn't work.* Or it may be that condition in your body has shackled you for so long you have told yourself to stop hoping, because if you don't get your hopes up, at least you won't be disappointed again. Maybe you think you are not qualified to pray because you just don't have "enough faith." You may have heard that you have to pray without doubt in your heart (Mark 11:23), but you can't help but feel fear as you are confronted with the size of the tumor, or how far the disease has spread, or the level of your platelet count.

So you have simply stopped praying. Stopped hoping. Stopped believing.

If any of what I have said seems all too familiar to you, I have a word for you. May I invite you to give the Lord another chance?

When God taught the Israelites to keep the first Passover, He said, "This month shall be your beginning of months." This speaks of a new beginning.

Today I want to encourage you to take a step of faith. Let this day be your beginning of days. When you put your trust in the Lamb who was slain for you, you are stepping into a new beginning. Forget the former things. Forget the failures and disappointments of the past.

I want to invite you to once again start putting your faith in the One who gave His life for you. Take up the bread and say, "Thank You, Lord Jesus. You gave Your body to be broken so mine might be whole. By the stripes that fell on Your back, I see my body healed from the crown of my head to the soles of my feet."

Take the cup in your hand and say, "Lord Jesus, thank You for Your precious blood that has washed me clean from every sin. Today I partake of every inheritance of the righteous, which includes protection, healing, wholeness, and provision."

As you come to the Lord's Table, trust that you will experience what the Israelites did after partaking of the roasted lamb and coming out with not one feeble and not one sick. My friend, I am believing with you for your breakthrough. The enemy wants to keep you bound, but the Lord wants to set you free!

TODAY'S THOUGHT

Perhaps you never had a revelation of how the Lord Jesus suffered to pay for your healing. Perhaps you never knew what power was contained in the holy Communion. But I pray that as you continue to meditate on the truths you are learning about in this book, the eyes of your understanding will be opened to the exceeding greatness of His power toward you, and you will know that the same power that raised Christ from the dead works for you (Eph. 1:18–20).

TODAY'S PRAYER

Lord Jesus, thank You that You are the God of new beginnings, new life, and a new future. I declare that my trust is in You, the

Lamb who was slain for me. I declare that I'm stepping into a brand-new beginning as I partake of the Communion today. I choose not to focus on past disappointments. I believe that the new has come and my breakthrough is at hand. Amen.

TESTIMONY

Enlarged Prostate Gland Reduced, Multiple Tumors Gone

A few years ago, my dad was diagnosed with an enlarged prostate. Doctors suspected cancer, but thankfully the biopsy came back negative. However, he was put on a treatment to manage his prostate condition and had to go for regular check-ups as his father had died of cancer.

Earlier this year, the doctors found further enlargement of my dad's prostate gland. Multiple tumors were also found in his femur (thigh bone). As a degree holder in bioengineering, I knew this was not a good sign as it could mean cancerous cells had spread to the bone marrow.

The doctors also suspected the same and wanted to do a full body scan for my dad. We also shared my dad's reports with my cousin, who is a renowned cancer consultant, and she concurred with the doctors. Fear gripped our hearts.

> WE PARTOOK OF THE HOLY COMMUNION EVERY NIGHT AND COULD FEEL A SENSE OF PEACE AND JOY.

I have been attending New Creation Church for over five years, and I listen to Pastor Prince's sermons over and over again. I have also read Pastor Prince's books and have been sharing his teachings with my family, who also watch his sermons on YouTube.

After we received the doctor's report, I video-called my parents, and we partook of the holy Communion together. We also held firm to God's healing promises. For the next few weeks, we continued to partake of the holy Communion every night and could feel a sense of peace and joy. My dad also stopped having fearful thoughts, and we declared that when the scan was done, the doctors would not find any tumors.

That was exactly what happened. The doctors and my cousin were baffled by the results. The doctors then asked my dad to do another scan and biopsy to confirm that he was in the clear. Praise God, once again, everything showed that my dad was in perfect health. Even his prostate gland had reduced in size. All this happened without any medical treatment.

Praise be to God!

Liam | Singapore

SECTION IV

FOR YOU, NOT AGAINST YOU

What then shall we say to these things? If God is for us, who can be against us? He who did not spare His own Son, but delivered Him up for us all, how shall He not with Him also freely give us all things? Who shall bring a charge against God's elect? It is God who justifies. Who is he who condemns? It is Christ who died, and furthermore is also risen, who is even at the right hand of God, who also makes intercession for us. . . . For I am persuaded that neither death nor life, nor angels nor principalities nor powers, nor things present nor things to come, nor height nor depth, nor any other created thing, shall be able to separate us from the love of God which is in Christ Jesus our Lord.

—Romans 8:31–34, 38–39

DAY 24
KNOW HIS WILL

"The thief does not come except to steal, and to kill, and to destroy. I have come that they may have life, and that they may have it more abundantly."

—John 10:10

I have shared with you some truths that I pray are burning in your heart right now. But maybe you are wondering if the disease you are fighting is somehow from God. Maybe you think He is punishing you for something you did and that there is a lesson He wants you to learn.

If you have believed any of the lies above, then you have fallen prey to Satan, who is the great deceiver and father of lies (Rev. 12:9; John 8:44 NLT). His *modus operandi* is to deceive you, and his master strategy is to convince you sickness is actually from God. I want you to know in no uncertain terms that your heavenly Father loves you, and He wants you well. He does not want your life to be cut short by sickness, and it is *never* His plan for you or your loved ones to suffer any sickness or disease.

I want you to be very clear on this: there is an enemy who wants to destroy you. Our Lord Jesus said that Satan has come to steal, kill, and destroy. Satan is a murderer (John 8:44). When Satan deceived Adam and Eve in the garden of Eden, sin came into the world. But man did not just lose his position of righteousness. We also lost our relationship with God and confidence in His heart for us. Fear and condemnation entered, robbing us of our faith and our trust in a good God.

Satan wants to steal from you your health, your youth, and your joy.

He wants to destroy every dream you have cherished and rip you from the embrace of the people in your life. He wants to kill you because he knows there is a call and purpose on your life that only you can fulfill, and he wants to find every way to snuff you out.

Every time you find yourself or your loved ones being robbed, be it of health, finances, or family relationships, God is *never* behind it. Man was created to enjoy everything God has provided, and that includes health. Our Lord Jesus said He came that we "may have life, and that they may have it more abundantly." When He said this, He wasn't simply referring to biological life. The Greek word used for *life* here is *zoe*, and it refers to the highest form of life, the life God lives by.[1] He does not want you to simply keep breathing. He came to give you a quality of life God Himself possesses, a life that is beyond ordinary human life.

Can you see His heart for you? He wants you to live a long, satisfying life full of His goodness, wholeness, and peace. That is His will for *you*!

TODAY'S THOUGHT

God's heart for you is found in His promise: "With long life I will satisfy him, and show him My salvation" (Ps. 91:16). The Hebrew word for *salvation* here is the word *yeshua*,[2] and that's the name of Jesus. God will satisfy you with a long, full life where you walk in all the blessings of health, wholeness, and provision you have in Christ. Whatever your circumstances might look like on the outside, keep standing on His promises.

TODAY'S PRAYER

Lord Jesus, thank You that You came that I might have life, and that I might have it more abundantly. Thank You that You defeated Satan at the cross. Your finished work has restored to me all that was lost in the fall. I believe it is Your will to give me a long, satisfying life full of the blessings of health, wholeness, and provision, and I receive them now by faith. Amen.

DAY 25

GOD'S HEART REVEALED

"He who has seen Me has seen the Father."

—John 14:9

How do you know it is God's will to heal you? Just look at what Jesus did during His earthly ministry. When we look at Jesus, we see our heavenly Father's heart for us, for Jesus said that anyone who has seen Him has seen the Father.

Throughout the Gospels, what do we see Jesus tirelessly doing?

And Jesus went about all Galilee, teaching in their synagogues, preaching the gospel of the kingdom, and healing all kinds of sickness and all kinds of disease among the people. Then His fame went throughout all Syria; and they brought to Him all sick people who were afflicted with various diseases and torments, and those who were demon-possessed, epileptics, and paralytics; and He healed them. (Matt. 4:23–24)

Then great multitudes came to Him, having with them the lame, blind, mute, maimed, and many others; and they laid them down at Jesus' feet, and He healed them. (Matt. 15:30)

When the sun was setting, all those who had any that were sick with various diseases brought them to Him; and He laid His hands on every one of them and healed them. (Luke 4:40)

Over and over again, the Bible records how our Lord Jesus "went about doing good and *healing all* who were oppressed by the devil" (Acts 10:38). He caused the lame to walk and the blind to see. He unstopped deaf ears. He cleansed people with leprosy. He even raised the dead.

And do you know what our Lord Jesus said about all that He did? He said, "The words I say to you I do not say on My own initiative or authority, but the Father, abiding continually in Me, does His works [His attesting miracles and acts of power]" (John 14:10 AMP).

Jesus said it was *the Father* who worked (through Him) wonderful healing miracles everywhere He went. Can you see that it is truly your heavenly Father's desire for you to be completely healed of every disease?

TODAY'S THOUGHT

Search the Scriptures and you will *never* find Jesus going through a village and saying to someone on the street, "Come here. You are too healthy. Receive some leprosy." You will never find Jesus saying, "My Father is chastising you, that's why you are sick." You know why? Because that is not in the heart of God. He does *not* give sicknesses and diseases. If there is a condition in your body, may you be confident of this: *God wants you well!*

TODAY'S PRAYER

Father God, thank You that Jesus perfectly reflects Your heart in every word He spoke and every healing and deliverance He worked. Thank You for showing me how much You want me free of sickness in every part of my body. I believe and declare that it is Your desire that I be completely healed of every disease and that I can confidently expect to receive the healing that I need. In Jesus' name, amen.

DAY 26

ONLY GOOD GIFTS

"If you then, being evil, know how to give good gifts to your children, how much more will your Father who is in heaven give good things to those who ask Him!"

—Matthew 7:11

As a father, it always pains me to see my children unwell. My firstborn daughter, Jessica, is all grown up now, but I remember how it broke my heart to see her bawling when she was suffering from viral fever as a baby. I remember cradling her in my arms and praying over her as I paced around her room the whole night. I sponged her feverish body over and over again. As long as she was sick, I could not rest. I hated the fever that was causing my baby to convulse in pain. I would have done anything to alleviate her discomfort. If I could have taken her fever in my own body so she would not have to go through the pain, I would gladly have done so.

What I feel when my children are unwell is only a microcosmic reflection of what our heavenly Father feels for us when we are unwell. He wants us brimming with health and life. He hates sicknesses and diseases because of what they do to us. But the difference is this: He was able to take our sicknesses, and He put them on Jesus' own body as He hung on the cross, so that we would not have to suffer them. The Bible tells us: "He Himself took our infirmities and bore our sicknesses" (Matt. 8:17).

Why did our Lord Jesus do that? Because He loves us so much. He could not rest until He had secured our salvation, our health, and our wholeness. Finally, when He had borne every sin, every disease, and every infirmity upon His own body, He cried, "It is finished!" (John 19:30) and rested.

The Bible shows us this clearly: God is a good God. He is our loving heavenly Father. That is why I cannot understand why there are those who teach that God sometimes uses sickness to teach us a lesson or that we need to "pray hard" for His healing. Can you imagine any earthly father inflicting suffering on his own child? Must you be persuaded to alleviate your child's pain? There are even some people who claim that it is sometimes God's will for us to be sick. But when their own children fall sick, they do everything within their power to ensure their children recover. If it were really God's will for us to be sick, seeking recovery would be deliberately trying to get out of God's will!

My friend, reject anything that even remotely suggests that God uses sickness and suffering to teach us something. Our Father is full of grace and mercy and wants us to be healthy, provided for, and protected from every evil occurrence, sickness, and disease!

TODAY'S THOUGHT

If earthly, fallible parents want the best for their children, how much more does our heavenly Father? He wants us strong, well, and enjoying life. Our Lord Jesus said if earthly fathers know how to give good gifts to their children, how much more does our heavenly Daddy (Matt. 7:11). Read this scripture again and again and open your heart to what it says about His love toward you. Today receive His abundant gift of healing.

TODAY'S PRAYER

Abba, Father, thank You that You are my Daddy God, and that You give only good gifts to Your children. Thank You for reminding me that You hate sickness and disease, and that You put them all on Jesus' body as He hung on the cross so that I would not have to suffer from them. Because the finished work of Jesus has secured my health, I am expecting Your healing to manifest in my body. Amen.

DAY 27
HE FREELY GIVES

He who did not spare His own Son, but delivered Him up for us all, how shall He not with Him also freely give us all things?

—Romans 8:32

Isaiah 53:5 tells us that by Jesus' stripes we are healed. Every stripe He bore as He was scourged was for our healing. And He willingly allowed stripe after stripe to rip into His body so you and I could be well. Don't ever believe the enemy's lie that God wants you sick or that He is not willing to heal you. At the cross, our Lord Jesus demonstrated once and for all that He wants you well.

The Bible even tells us that it pleased the Lord to "crush Him" (Isa. 53:10 NASB). I used to wonder how it could have pleased the Lord to crush His own Son. Then one day, the Lord showed me.

My wife, Wendy, and I had gone to a mall and the nearest parking lot we could find was quite a distance away. We did a lot of shopping that day and before we knew it, we had our hands full of shopping bags. By this time, our Jessica, who was a cherubic two-year-old then, was tired and wanted to be carried. I picked her up with one arm, and she was so exhausted she fell asleep on my shoulder almost immediately.

As we walked toward our car, I felt my arm go to sleep, and I realized the car was much farther away than I had thought. It felt like a million pins and needles were piercing my arm, and I knew I could stop the burning pain by simply putting Jessica down and making her walk the rest of the way. But she was sleeping so soundly and deeply, I could not bear to put her down. I loved her so much I was willing to "crush" my arm so my little darling could continue to sleep.

All of a sudden I began to understand how it could please God to crush Jesus, who is described in the same chapter as "the arm of the LORD" (Isa. 53:1). It pleased the Lord to crush His only begotten Son because of His great love for you and me. That was the only way God could save us from sin and disease, and He willingly chose to give up His Son.

Today you can have full assurance God wants to heal you. The Bible tells us, "He who did not spare His own Son, but delivered Him up for us all, how shall He not with Him also freely give us all things?"

God already gave us the best of heaven when He gave us His darling Jesus. What are our temporal needs when He has already given us a gift that is eternal? Whatever your needs are, whether it is financial provision or healing for your body, they are all lesser compared to the gift of His Son. How shall He not with Him also freely give them to you?

TODAY'S THOUGHT

If God did not withhold His own Son from you, He surely will not withhold His healing from you. In fact, He has already paid the price for your healing. Whatever it is you need in your life, your Father has already given to you all things through Jesus. Your part is to keep believing and keep trusting until you see the full manifestation of your healing.

TODAY'S PRAYER

Father, thank You that You willingly chose to give up Your only beloved Son because of Your great love for me. Thank You that

You gave me the best of heaven when Jesus was crushed to save me from sin and disease. The price has been paid and healing is mine today. I believe and trust in You for a full manifestation of Your health and wholeness. In Jesus' name, amen.

DAY 28

HIS PERFECT WILL, HIS FINAL WORD

"Our Father in heaven, hallowed be Your name. Your kingdom come. Your will be done on earth as it is in heaven."

—Matthew 6:9–10

I want to share with you a precious testimony from Caleb, a father in Texas who wrote to my team:

My youngest son was diagnosed with scoliosis when his X-ray showed a seventeen-degree curve in his spine. Upon receiving the news, fear, doubt, anger, sadness, worry, and condemnation began to set in our hearts. We were also concerned about potential disabilities and surgeries for our son in the future.

As a pastor, I found myself struggling with my Christian beliefs. Nevertheless, I could feel the Lord's loving embrace and peace as I prayed for my son. My church also prayed for him, and we believed the Lord could, and would, heal him.

The doctor referred him to a children's hospital and arranged for an appointment. By faith, we decided to go for the appointment to confirm the healing had already begun. Even though doubt, condemnation, and fear crept into our hearts, we kept declaring the finished work of the cross and we kept partaking of the holy Communion.

During the appointment, the doctor examined my son and took more X-rays. Then she said, "I have good news for you!" and showed us the X-rays that displayed no trace of scoliosis. Our son's spine had straightened out. The Lord had healed him! There is victory and power in the cross indeed!

We now distribute a copy of Pastor Prince's book The Power of Right Believing *to every new member in our church. We believe miracles happen as we fill ourselves with the good news of the gospel.*

I really felt for Caleb when he described the feelings he went through on hearing his son was diagnosed with a condition that could potentially lead to lifelong disability. Every loving parent wants their child to be well and to enjoy a quality life, and that's also our heavenly Father's heart and will toward us.

Despite his fears and uncertainties, Caleb did the best thing he could for his son. He kept declaring the finished work of the cross, and he kept partaking of the holy Communion. And just like that, with nothing spectacular happening, no voice booming out from heaven, and no earth-shaking demonstration of power, his son was healed. Are you also concerned about a health issue today? I pray that as you do what Caleb did, you will also see God's supernatural healing manifest for you!

TODAY'S THOUGHT

If you have been told you will die young or don't have long to live, I want you to know you don't have to accept the diagnosis. Thank God for doctors who have dedicated their lives to alleviating pain and suffering, but with all due respect, they don't have the final word in our lives—the almighty God does. He is the Alpha and Omega, the First and the Last (Rev. 22:13), and He can override any grim diagnosis, any death report.

TODAY'S PRAYER

Father in heaven, thank You that no matter what diagnosis I may have received, I don't have to be afraid of it. You have the final say, and Your Word declares that healing is Your will for me and that I am healed by Jesus' stripes. I'm just going to keep declaring the finished work of the cross and keep partaking of the holy Communion. I believe Your healing power is working in my body even now. Amen.

DAY 29

BE ROOTED IN HIS LOVE

That you, being rooted and grounded in love, may be able to comprehend with all the saints what is the width and length and depth and height—to know the love of Christ which passes knowledge.

—Ephesians 3:17–19

My friend, if you have received a negative medical report, it is natural for you to be fearful. Notice that in yesterday's testimony, Caleb felt fear, doubt, anger, sadness, worry, and condemnation, and he even "struggled with his Christian beliefs." The Lord does not expect you to never be shaken. But in the midst of your tumult of emotions, keep your eyes on Jesus and keep on declaring His finished work over your situation.

Maybe right now you are angry with God for allowing a disease to take root in the body of a loved one. Maybe you are feeling helpless because it feels as if you are standing on the sidelines, and there is nothing you can do to alleviate the suffering. Or maybe you yourself have been confined to a hospital bed, and you are terrified. Every time you are wheeled out for more scans, you don't know what the doctors will find, and you are crying out, "God, why is this happening to me? Where are You?"

When you are staring at the symptoms in your body or in the body of your loved one, when it seems as though you have prayed with all your heart and still the sickness remains, I know it is hard to believe God can heal. Or maybe you believe He can heal, but you doubt He wants to.

Perhaps you have given up hope because you think that if He wanted to heal you or your loved one, He would have done it already.

If that is how you feel right now, may I encourage you to *feed on His love for you.* The doubts in your mind might be screaming so loudly it's hard for you to even believe in Him anymore. But I pray that you will be able to catch a fresh glimpse of the width and length and depth and height of your Savior's love for you (Eph. 3:18–19). I pray that even when your mind cannot understand it, your heart will be rooted and established in His love for you. When you are so established in His love, you will see Him do exceedingly, abundantly, above all that you ask or think (Eph. 3:20).

Do not allow the enemy to shake your faith. Do not allow the enemy to sell you any more lies. He is a defeated foe, and whatever evil he meant against you, God will turn it around for your good and for His glory. The Word of God declares that "*no weapon formed against you shall prosper*" (Isa. 54:17). Even if the enemy has formed some weapon of disease against you, rest assured that it has no power to prevail against you.

TODAY'S THOUGHT

You have a heavenly Father who loves you so much He gave up His own Son for you. The devil wants you to be disillusioned and to turn away from God, but *now* is the time you need to turn to your Savior and trust Him more than ever before. Now is the time for you to take your authority as a child of the Most High God, and to claim every promise in the Scriptures of health and long life that Jesus died to give you!

TODAY'S PRAYER

Lord Jesus, thank You for loving me so unconditionally. I stand on Your unfailing promise that no weapon of sickness formed against me shall prosper. Thank You that nothing the enemy brings against me, whether it is sickness, fear, or any kind of oppression, has power over my life. My eyes are on You, Jesus, and I will keep declaring and resting in Your finished work. Amen.

SECTION V

NO PLACE FOR FEAR

He who dwells in the secret place of the Most High
Shall abide under the shadow of the Almighty.
I will say of the Lord, "He is my refuge and my fortress;
My God, in Him I will trust."
Surely He shall deliver you from the snare of the fowler
And from the perilous pestilence.
He shall cover you with His feathers,
And under His wings you shall take refuge;
His truth shall be your shield and buckler.
You shall not be afraid of the terror by night,
Nor of the arrow that flies by day,
Nor of the pestilence that walks in darkness,
Nor of the destruction that lays waste at noonday.

—Psalm 91:1–6

DAY 30

FOCUS ON HIS PROMISES

God has not given us a spirit of fear, but of power and of love and of a sound mind.

—2 Timothy 1:7

Down through the years, as I minister to precious people, I have seen how fear can creep in when someone is diagnosed with a condition or when loved ones develop serious illnesses. If you know someone who is experiencing this, you can encourage them with the promise in the verse above. Because of what Jesus did on the cross, we do not have to remain apprehensive, but can trust the Lord to come to a place where there is no room in our hearts for fear, knowing that His perfect love drives out every fear (1 John 4:18).

I understand that finding out you or your loved one has a medical condition can be frightening. Maybe you have just discovered in your body a lump that was never there before, or you can no longer ignore worrying symptoms like the pain that won't go away. Maybe you have already been given a diagnosis and it is worse than what you had imagined. Now it feels like you cannot breathe, and you are trying your best not to panic, but it is so hard.

Fear can overwhelm you like a tsunami. It can paralyze you. It can cause you to become angry. Angry at life. At God. At everyone. Maybe you know exactly what I mean. If you do, may I ask you to please read on? I believe the Lord has a word for you.

The tumor, the dialysis machine, and the feeding tube are real.

But it is so important for you to know this: the power of God is even *more* real.

The enemy wants you to be intensely focused on the disease, the devastating medical report, the incessant beeping of the monitors around you, and the sterile smell of the hospital room. He wants you to be completely fixated on the fears and questions that keep screaming in your mind so you are effectively blinded to the truth of what God has done. As long as all you can see is your pain, your dread, your disappointment, and your suffering, he has the upper hand.

Why is he so bent on keeping you absorbed in the challenge you are facing? Because he is afraid you will see he has already been defeated. The Bible tells us that at the cross, our Lord Jesus disarmed all principalities and powers, made a public spectacle of them, and triumphed over them (Col. 2:15). The enemy has been stripped of his weapons (this includes all kinds of sickness and disease) against you. You do not need to fear him, child of the Most High!

TODAY'S THOUGHT

The devil will keep trying to deceive and distract you from the truth of his defeat. He will keep trying to get you to focus on the temporal, visible things around you. He does not want you to see the things that are eternal—like the angels that have been instructed to watch over you and keep you in all your ways (Ps. 91:11), or like the Word of God that will never pass away (Matt. 24:35) and declares that by His stripes *you are healed* (Isa. 53:5). My friend, look to the cross of Jesus. The devil has been disarmed. Fear has no place in your heart. Hallelujah!

TODAY'S PRAYER

Lord Jesus, thank You that because You disarmed all principalities and powers, stripped the enemy of his weapons, and triumphed over them at the cross, I need not fear any sickness or disease. Thank You for giving me a spirit of power and of love and of a sound mind. Thank You for driving out every fear as I meditate on Your promises and Your perfect love for me. Amen.

DAY 31

MORE WITH YOU THAN AGAINST YOU

You are of God, little children, and have overcome them, because He who is in you is greater than he who is in the world.

—1 John 4:4

When you or a loved one faces a frightening medical condition, questions for which you have no answers can often overwhelm your mind. *What are we going to do? How long do I have? Who will look after my kids? How am I going to afford the treatment? Will I ever be the same? Why me?* What can you do when your thoughts are completely out of control and you can only imagine the worst is coming?

The Bible records the following account in 2 Kings 6 for our encouragement. Israel's enemies were so desperate to capture the prophet Elisha that they sent a great army with horses and chariots by night and surrounded the city where he was staying. When Elisha's servant woke up and saw this army, he despaired and cried out in fear, "What shall we do?"

May I invite you to read for yourself what happened next?

> *So he [Elisha] answered,* "Do not fear, for those who are with us are more than those who are with them." *And Elisha prayed, and said, "Lord, I pray, open his eyes that he may see." Then the Lord opened the eyes of the young man, and he saw. And behold, the*

> *mountain was full of horses and chariots of fire all around Elisha. (2 Kings 6:16–17)*

It may feel like a formidable army of symptoms, negative reports, and maybe even financial debt has surrounded you. But, beloved, do not fear, for those who are *with you* are *so much more* than those who are with them.

Right now, I pray that the Lord will open your eyes so you might see the legions of angels stationed around you. Take your eyes off your enemies. The ability of your enemies to hurt you is *nothing* compared to the greatness of your God and His power to save you. Take your eyes off the enemy so you may see the exceeding greatness of God's power toward you. The same mighty power that raised our Lord Jesus from the grave, the same power that seated Him at God's right hand in the heavenly places—*far above* all principalities, power, might, and dominion, and *every name* that is named, not only in this age but also in the age to come (Eph. 1:19–21)—is working *for* you and for your loved one!

Is human papillomavirus a name? Is bacterial meningitis a name? Is Parkinson's disease a name? Then it has to yield to Jesus, who is seated at the Father's right hand, far above the diseases. And because you are in Christ today, as He is, so are you in this world (1 John 4:17)!

TODAY'S THOUGHT

Today you might not physically see angels, but I pray you will know that the Lord's army of angels is with you, ministering protection and healing to you (Heb. 1:14). When the enemy tries to keep you focused on your symptoms and pain, choose to see your loving Savior with you and fighting this battle *for you*. Our confidence is not in what we see in the natural but in the exceeding greatness of His power that is working supernaturally in us and for us!

TODAY'S PRAYER

Father God, open my eyes that I may see Your angels surrounding me on every side. I declare that those who are with me are greater than those who are against me. Thank You that [say the name of your condition] must yield to the mighty name of Jesus. I believe that as He is seated at Your right hand, far above every sickness and disease, so am I in this world because I am in Him. No sickness can nor will prevail against me. In Jesus' mighty name, amen.

DAY 32

CAST OUT FEAR

Keep yourselves in the love of God.

—Jude 1:21

As you wait for the doctor's verdict on the nature of those cells he saw in your scan, or as you look at the dark mass on your X-ray, you can't help but be filled with trepidation. You try telling yourself not to be fearful, but you can't seem to stop fearing. Do you know why? Because you cannot reason your way out of fear. Fear is not logical.

The only way to get fear out of your life is to cast it out, and the Bible tells us how:

> *There is no fear in love; but* perfect love casts out fear, *because fear involves torment. (1 John 4:18)*

You cast out fear by exposing yourself to the perfect love of God. Keep allowing His love to inundate you and drive out every fear. The Bible talks about keeping ourselves in the love of God. Instead of focusing on the pain in your body or the sickness causing your loved one to suffer, keep yourself in His love. Set your mind on the infallible, inexhaustible, and perfect love of your heavenly Father.

You have a God who loves you so much He gave His Son to die on the cross for you. That, my friend, is why you can always have rock-solid assurance you are loved by Him. The Bible defines His love for us like this:

> *God showed how much he loved us by sending his one and only Son into the world so that we might have eternal life through him. This is real love—not that we loved God, but that he loved us and sent his Son as a sacrifice to take away our sins. (1 John 4:9–10 NLT)*

The cross is everlasting proof of God's love for you. The cross is the measure of how much He loves you. You must never judge His love based on your circumstances. The devil can attack your circumstances, but he can never attack the cross. Take your eyes off your circumstances and put them on the cross. That's where God's love for you was demonstrated once and for all.

TODAY'S THOUGHT

No matter how dark and dire your circumstances may be right now, know that the Father's perfect love for you is greater. Keep allowing it to inundate you and drive out every fear. As you meditate on His infallible and inexhaustible love for you demonstrated at the cross, He will turn your circumstances around for your good. Let your heart find rest and peace in the security of His love.

TODAY'S PRAYER

Father, thank You that You are showing me Your perfect love unveiled through Your giving of Your darling Son to die on the cross for me. Thank You that Your love is rock solid and never based on my circumstances. I set my mind and heart on Your infallible, inexhaustible, and perfect love to cast out all my fears. Amen.

DAY 33

ABIDE IN HIS PERFECT LOVE

Because you have made the Lord, *who is*
my refuge,
Even the Most High, your dwelling place,
No evil shall befall you,
Nor shall any plague come near your dwelling.

—Psalm 91:9–10

I know it can be very hard to *feel* God's love for you when you are faced with multiple symptoms in your body, mounting debts from your medical bills, and worries about your future. We live in a world where we are governed by our five senses, and there are times when it is hard to believe in the love of Someone we can't see, touch, or hear. But we cannot depend on feelings and outward circumstances (that can change) to be assured of God's love for us. It is so important we fix our eyes, instead, on our Lord Jesus, whose love for us is perfect, never changes, and never fails.

Today and over the following two days, may I share with you some of the things you can do that I believe will help to keep you in His perfect love?

Instead of allowing the enemy to feed you with lies that cause you to be fearful, keep listening to messages that will keep you in the consciousness of God's love for you. Embrace His love to drive out every fear. Every time the enemy tries to attack you with fears, plug into a sermon that magnifies the Lord's goodness and love for you. Instead of giving in to the devices of the enemy, keep listening to sermons about Jesus' finished work.

Instead of reading articles on the internet that tell you how serious your condition can become, or reading your medical report over and over again, read praise reports about the Lord's love and faithfulness.[1] Read scriptures about His love and healing promises. Garrison yourself with the Word of God and keep yourself in His love.

The Bible tells us, "And we have *known and believed* the love that God has for us. God is love, and *he who abides in love abides in God*, and God in him" (1 John 4:16). It's not enough to know verses *about* His love. Keep meditating on them until you *believe* He loves you. When we keep ourselves in the consciousness of God's love, we are abiding in God. In other words, we are making Him our dwelling place. That is so powerful because when the Lord is your dwelling place, you are in a place of safety and protection.

Read Psalm 91 and declare over yourself that no evil shall befall you nor shall any plague come near your dwelling. As you abide in Him, the almighty God becomes your refuge and fortress. It doesn't matter how many people have died from the disease you have been diagnosed with. A thousand may fall at your side and ten thousand at your right hand, but it shall not come near you (Ps. 91:7). And even if you are already in trouble, the Lord is with you and He will deliver you.

TODAY'S THOUGHT

No matter what you are facing, you can make the Lord your dwelling place. The more you abide in His love, the more God Himself becomes your refuge and fortress of protection. There is safety and protection when you draw near to Him and dwell in His sweet presence, His love, and His Word. Fear will go as you meditate on how He is with you even in your day of trouble, strengthening and delivering you.

TODAY'S PRAYER

Father in heaven, I'm running to You and to the safety of Your love for me. In Your love is my dwelling place, my refuge, and my fortress. Thank You for Your sweet presence, Your Word, and Your promises. I believe You are with me and You will deliver me from all fear and from anything that is troubling my body and health. Amen.

DAY 34

RECEIVE HIS HEALING POWER

When we bless the cup at the Lord's Table, aren't we sharing in the blood of Christ? And when we break the bread, aren't we sharing in the body of Christ?

—1 Corinthians 10:16 NLT

In the previous reading I shared with you some of the things you can do that I believe will help to keep you in God's love and drive fear out of your life. Here is another powerful step to take: whenever fear tries to creep up on you, go somewhere quiet and meditate on how much the Lord loves you as you partake of the holy Communion.

Right off, you might be wondering, *If God loves me, why do I have to pray or partake of the Communion at all? What difference does that make? And if it's His will to heal me, why am I not automatically healed?*

May I first answer the question of why you are not healed automatically? My friend, we know it is God's will for everyone to receive salvation, to receive the gift of eternal life that was freely given to the world (John 3:16). But we all have the choice to accept or reject God's offer. Nobody gets saved "automatically." God is a gentleman, and He will not force His salvation on anyone. He will not force His gifts or blessings on us. He will not force His health or goodness on us.

So what difference does prayer and partaking of the holy Communion make? When we pray and partake of the holy Communion, we are actively releasing our faith to be aligned with God's will, God's Word, and God's power. We are not begging Him to heal us or trying to persuade Him to heal our loved ones—we already know it is His will to heal. Prayer is about building an intimate relationship with Him. When we pray and partake of the holy Communion, we are receiving His love for us and receiving His healing power into our physical bodies. Talk to God today (that's what prayer is) about your health challenges, and let Him impart boldness to you and confidence in your heart that He wants you healthy.

So when fear grips your heart, go somewhere quiet and find rest in the intimate love of Jesus through the holy Communion. Talk to your Savior, and as you lift up the bread, tell Him, "Lord Jesus, thank You that You love me so much You allowed Your body to be broken so mine can be whole. Right now, I receive Your wholeness, Your strength, and Your divine health." As you lift up the cup, say, "Thank You for Your precious blood, which has cleansed me of every sin. Right now, I can come boldly to Your throne of grace, knowing I am completely righteous, knowing my prayers avail much!"

TODAY'S THOUGHT

Remember that when you partake of the Communion, you are "proclaiming the Lord's death" (1 Cor. 11:26) and reminding the devil and his cohorts of their humiliating defeat at the cross (Col. 2:15). You are proclaiming to the enemy that he has *no* right to put symptoms or sicknesses on your body because your Lord Jesus has already borne every disease and pain on His own body and qualified you for your healing. So partake boldly and receive the healing, health, and life He went to the cross to give you!

TODAY'S PRAYER

Thank You, Lord Jesus, that I can come boldly and partake of all the blessings and healing power of Your broken body and shed blood. Thank You that it is Your will for me to be healed and that You have already qualified me for healing and divine health. I believe and declare that sickness has no right to remain in my body. Amen.

DAY 35

FIX YOUR EYES ON JESUS

"For we have no power to face this vast army that is attacking us. We do not know what to do, but our eyes are on you."

—2 Chronicles 20:12 NIV

In the past two readings I have shared with you some of the things you can do to keep yourself in God's love. I pray these powerful truths are beginning to help you see how you can effectively drive fear out of your life and keep it out. Here is another precious truth that will garrison your heart and mind from the enemy's lies.

Take time to worship the Lord, *especially* when it feels like overwhelming odds are against you. Do what King Jehoshaphat did when his enemies joined forces and amassed a formidable army to destroy Israel. In the natural, Jehoshaphat knew Israel had no chance of winning the battle. But he chose to do something you and I need to learn to do whenever we are besieged by our enemies. He cried out to the Lord, saying, "*We do not know what to do, but our eyes are on you*" (2 Chron. 20:12 NIV). Jehoshaphat then placed not commandos but worshipers at the head of his army, and this is what they sang: "Give thanks to the LORD, for *his love endures forever*" (2 Chron. 20:21 NIV).

Instead of despairing because of their enemies, they chose to fix their eyes on the Lord, giving thanks to Him and singing of His love. This happened long before the cross of Jesus. How much more can you and I sing of His love, which never fails, which endures forever!

And do you know what happened? The Lord defeated Israel's enemies by turning them against each other, and Jehoshaphat's troops did not even have to lift a finger to fight. Instead, when they came to the place that was supposed to be their battleground, their enemies were already dead, and all they ended up doing was collecting so much plunder that it took them three days to collect it all.

In Jesus' name, may this happen to you too. When you are overwhelmed by challenges, and you don't know what to do or even how to feel, just cry out to the Lord and tell Him, "Lord, I don't know what to do, but my eyes are on You." That's the most powerful posture you can take, with your eyes fixed not on your enemies but on your Savior. As you focus on His love that endures forever, the Lord Himself will fight your battle for you (2 Chron. 20:15). May you be so conscious of His perfect love that every fear is driven from your life, and may you walk away so much stronger than before your enemies tried to come against you!

TODAY'S THOUGHT

Beloved, our Lord Jesus tells us, "The very hairs of your head are all numbered. Do not fear therefore" (Luke 12:7). Your Daddy God loves you so much and cares about every minute detail of your life. There is nothing too big or too small for Him. If it matters to you, it matters to Him. Every time you are fearful, fix your eyes on Him and His love, and watch Him fight your battles.

TODAY'S PRAYER

Father God, thank You for Your great love for me. I give You everything that is troubling me today. I give You all my fears.

I choose to fix my eyes on You, give thanks to You, and sing of Your love that endures forever. I believe that You care about every part of my body and will bring to nothing all the enemy tries to do against me. In Jesus' name, amen.

DAY 36

COME BACK TO SIMPLICITY

But I fear, lest somehow, as the serpent deceived Eve by his craftiness, so your minds may be corrupted from the simplicity that is in Christ.

—2 Corinthians 11:3

As I was writing *Eat Your Way to Life and Health*, the Lord began to speak to me about healing in a very strong way. He led me to read a verse I believe articulates clearly His will for us. It was written by the disciple whom Jesus loved, the disciple who was an eyewitness as Jesus went about healing all who came to Him, the disciple who leaned on Jesus' bosom and knew the heartbeat of His love:

> *Beloved, I pray that you may prosper in all things* and be in health, *just as your soul prospers. (3 John 1:2)*

What I want you to see is this: John was writing to the well-beloved Gaius, a believer. John knew that Gaius's soul was already prospering. If you have invited Jesus into your heart to be your Lord and Savior, then you have received the gift of eternal life and can have full assurance that heaven is your home (Rom. 10:9–11). Whatever challenges you might be faced with on the outside, your soul, which is eternal, has begun prospering. But it wasn't enough for John to know Gaius's soul was prospering. John prayed that Gaius would also "prosper in all things and be in health." In other words, you can pray for your outward, physical body to be healthy even as your soul is healthy in Christ.

You can be sure God's will is for you to be healthy because His Word declares it. Since His will is for you to be "in health," don't go with human tradition or man's opinion that says it is sometimes His will for you to be sick. Don't let man's conjectures and theories cause you to believe the lie that maybe God wants you to endure the sickness in your body so you can learn to trust Him more or grow in patience. Because of what Jesus did at Calvary, we can be sure sickness is *never* from God. Healing is!

Come back to the simplicity of declaring like a child, "Jesus loves me, this I know, for the Bible tells me so." In the same way, how do I know Jesus wants us walking in His health and wholeness? For the Bible tells me so.

TODAY'S THOUGHT

The power of God's Word to break the fears that paralyze and hold you back from enjoying health is simple. It is the Lord Jesus. The simple truth is that Christ is your Savior, your healer, your provider, your peace, and your forgiveness. He is your "I AM" (Ex. 3:14). That means that if you are feeling sick or weak today, He is saying to you, "I am your healer. I am your strength." When you keep your eyes on Jesus and His Word, the enemy's lies and attacks cannot keep you in fear or in bondage to any sickness or disease.

TODAY'S PRAYER

Beautiful Lord Jesus, thank You that You are my loving Savior, my healer, my provider, my peace, and my forgiveness. Thank You that Your Word tells me that it is Your desire for me to be walking in health and wholeness. I simply declare that You are the great "I AM" for my every need, and therefore I will not be afraid. I receive from Your heart of love every kind of practical supply I need today. Amen.

DAY 37
NO IMPOSSIBILITIES

"The things which are impossible with men are possible with God."

—Luke 18:27

Let me share with you a praise report from Kathy, whose husband, Marcus, had been diagnosed with Alzheimer's, a progressive brain disease that worsens over time and has no cure. I can only imagine the helplessness and fear Marcus and Kathy felt when they first received the diagnosis. But read on and see what the Lord did for them:

Some years ago, Marcus's doctor told us that, based on his latest brain scan as well as scans from his hospital stay fourteen months earlier following a brain bleed, Marcus had Alzheimer's disease. She told us that Marcus should "get his affairs in order" and begin to plan to retire permanently from his job.

Needless to say, this was a huge shock to us—one that neither of us was ready or willing to accept. But we truly gave the situation to God. There is much to say about the journey our Lord took us on, one that included your teaching as confirmation of what we believed we were hearing from Him.

Our Daddy God gave us faith, hope, and such peace during those dark times as we began to really trust Him with every aspect of our lives. It was through Scripture and your messages about the holy Communion that prompted us to begin taking the

Communion at home on a regular basis. We believe that was when our future began to brighten.

Did you notice they didn't simply accept the shocking diagnosis? They filled themselves with scriptures, kept listening to the preached Word, and started partaking of the holy Communion at home on a regular basis. As they did all that, their "future began to brighten." They might have continued to see symptoms during that time, but they persisted. Today they know their breakthrough began when they started partaking of the Communion regularly. It wasn't immediate and complete, but it *began* then.

Kathy wrote on to say that four-and-a-half years later, Marcus underwent another MRI, and as his neurosurgeon studied the scan, she looked quite perplexed. Then she said, "I'm looking at a very healthy brain. There is no Alzheimer's disease here. I'm removing that diagnosis completely from your medical records."

The things that are impossible with man are possible with our God (Luke 18:27)! Instead of degenerating, Marcus's brain became "very healthy," and he was completely discharged of Alzheimer's disease. Hallelujah!

TODAY'S THOUGHT

No matter what diagnosis you might have received, keep partaking of the Communion, filling your heart with scriptures, and listening to messages about the Lord's finished work. Keep remembering our Lord Jesus and His love for you. Each time fear threatens to consume you, run into His arms of love again and allow His love to cast out every fear. And even if you don't see your breakthrough happening yet, keep fighting the good fight of faith, knowing in your heart God loves you and wants you well. What He did for Marcus, He can do for you too!

TODAY'S PRAYER

Daddy God, thank You that absolutely nothing is impossible with You. Thank You that You are never too busy to hear my cries and to come to my help. As I partake of the Communion today, I believe Your miracle-working power is driving out every symptom of sickness in my body and infusing me with Your divine strength and life. Amen.

SECTION VI

HE PAID THE BILL

And you, being dead in your trespasses and the uncircumcision of your flesh, He has made alive together with Him, having forgiven you all trespasses, having wiped out the handwriting of requirements that was against us, which was contrary to us. And He has taken it out of the way, having nailed it to the cross. Having disarmed principalities and powers, He made a public spectacle of them, triumphing over them in it.

—Colossians 2:13–15

DAY 38
JEHOVAH JIREH

Abraham called the name of the place, The-Lord-Will-Provide [Jehovah Jireh].

—Genesis 22:14

If you or your loved one has been diagnosed with a medical condition, chances are, you are also being confronted with mounting medical bills. Maybe your take-home pay is just enough to cover your monthly living expenses and what you have been diagnosed with has put a strain on your finances. You have maxed out your credit cards to pay for hospitalization, medication, and all the scans you had to undergo, and you are now mired in debt. Perhaps you have no health insurance because you are between jobs and cannot afford it. And now, you have not seen a doctor as the potential cost of seeing one worries you even more than your condition.

Did you know the Bible records the story of a woman who found herself in a serious financial crisis because of her long-term health condition (Mark 5:25–34)? She suffered from a hemorrhage or "flow of blood" and had been constantly bleeding for twelve long years. We also know she had gone to many doctors in her bid to be cured and had endured much suffering at their hands. Over the years, she spent everything she had to pay for her treatments, but her condition only grew worse.

As you read this, maybe you can identify with this woman's predicament. Maybe you have been battling a medical condition for years, and your bank account has been completely depleted because of undergoing all the treatments the experts said would help you get better but haven't. Perhaps the ballooning debt has you discouraged to the point of giving up. In the following two readings, I want to share more of this woman's story with you, but let me first give you a word about your finances.

Beloved, do not be dismayed by all the accumulating bills. The Lord is not just *Jehovah Rapha*, the Lord your healer, He is also *Jehovah Jireh*, the Lord your provider. The Bible promises that He "will liberally supply (fill until full) your every need according to His riches in glory in Christ Jesus" (Phil. 4:19 AMP). I pray that you will be so much more conscious of the abundance of His inexhaustible supply than of the demands on your finances. Don't ever feel like you have to handle the pressures all by yourself and take care of all the medical bills while ensuring your family has food to eat. Do not worry, for your heavenly Father knows you need all these things (Matt. 6:32). Let go of your worries and keep your eyes on Him. He will take care of you.

TODAY'S THOUGHT

As you cast your cares to the Lord and allow Him to be your *Jehovah Jireh*, you can receive the peace He gives. Today hear your Lord Jesus whispering to you, "Peace I leave with you, My peace I give to you; not as the world gives do I give to you. Let not your heart be troubled, neither let it be afraid" (John 14:27). As you receive His supernatural peace and rest in His love for you, you will see Him liberally provide for you and your family all that you need.

TODAY'S PRAYER

Lord Jesus, thank You that You are my *Jehovah Jireh*, the Lord my provider. Thank You for Your promise to liberally supply my every need according to Your riches in glory. I receive Your supernatural peace that surpasses my understanding to guard my heart and mind from all fears. And I receive Your abundant and practical provision for every need. Amen.

DAY 39

LET FAITH ARISE

She had heard about Jesus, so she came up behind him through the crowd and touched his robe.

—*Mark 5:27* NLT

In yesterday's reading, I started to describe the condition of the woman who had suffered greatly for twelve years from a hemorrhage. She had not only spent all her money to pay for treatments that did not help her, but her condition had grown worse.

Perhaps you have been put through so many tests, been subject to so many probes, and tried so many "revolutionary cures," you have lost count. But each time the treatment failed, and all you are left with is more bills and a condition that has deteriorated despite your best efforts. You may have come to the point where you are tired of trying and tired of hoping. The disease has ravaged your body and you have neither the will nor the finances to continue fighting.

If that describes you, please know it is not by coincidence you are reading these words. I believe the Lord wanted you to read this because He loves you. Do not give up. Even if you have gone to specialist after specialist and tried various treatments to no avail, there is still hope!

I really believe what I am about to share will help you receive your breakthrough both in your body and in your finances. Here is the apostle Mark's account:

When she heard about Jesus, she came behind Him in the crowd

> *and touched His garment. For she said, "If only I may touch His clothes, I shall be made well." Immediately the fountain of her blood was dried up, and she felt in her body that she was healed of the affliction. . . . And He said to her, "Daughter, your faith has made you well. Go in peace, and be healed of your affliction." (Mark 5:27–29, 34)*

If you have been believing God for healing, you might be thinking, *If only I could see Jesus with my own eyes or hear Him with my own ears, then I could be healed.* The apostle Luke recorded that "great multitudes came together to hear, and to be healed by Him" (Luke 5:15). These multitudes heard Jesus themselves, and they were healed.

But the apostle Mark's account about the woman with the issue of blood doesn't say, "When she heard Jesus." It says, "When she heard *about* Jesus."

Hallelujah! Do you know what that means? It means we can have the same faith this woman had just by hearing *about* Jesus. We may not see or hear Jesus in person as the multitudes did. But just by hearing *about* Jesus, we can receive the same faith and healing breakthrough the woman did—even if the conditions have been in our bodies for years, and even if doctors and expensive treatments have failed!

TODAY'S THOUGHT

Faith as defined in God's Word is "the confidence that what we hope for will actually happen" (Heb. 11:1 NLT). Faith for any breakthrough or healing in your life springs forth when you hear about Jesus and His goodness and grace. And the more you hear about His finished work on the cross, the more faith will arise in you to receive your miracle.

TODAY'S PRAYER

Lord Jesus, thank You that the more I hear about Your goodness and grace, the more faith is arising in my heart. Thank You that because of Your finished work on the cross, I can confidently expect to receive my healing breakthrough. I rest in Your love for me and thank You for the healing You are working in my body. Amen.

DAY 40
WHAT ARE YOU HEARING?

Faith comes from hearing, and hearing by the word of Christ.

—Romans 10:17 NASB

Allow me to show you one more thing from the story of the woman in Mark 5 whom Jesus healed from a "flow of blood" that had caused her great suffering for twelve years. We saw in the last reading that her miracle began when she "heard about Jesus." What do you think the woman heard about Jesus that was so powerful?

For twelve years she had been bleeding. According to Levitical law, she was "unclean." Whoever touched her or even touched anything she had sat on was also considered unclean (Lev. 15:19–25). This means for twelve years she had been shunned and ostracized. For twelve years she was not allowed to touch anyone so she would not defile them. Can you imagine living a life where every single day, you are painfully reminded of how unclean, how impure, and how disqualified you are?

But then she heard something about Jesus.

She heard something that caused hope to spring up in her jaded heart and gave her the faith to believe she would be made well simply by touching His clothes.

She heard something that gave her the boldness and resolve to press her weakened body through an entire crowd, even though Levitical law forbade her from touching anyone.

Most of all, she heard something that caused her to believe that in spite of the fact she was unclean, she could receive healing. That is what I want you to hear about our Lord Jesus today.

In spite of the fact you are unclean, in spite of the fact you have failed, in spite of the fact there is sin in your life, *you can receive healing*!

Don't allow man's traditions to keep you away from your loving Savior. Come to Him just as you are. You do not need to do anything to qualify yourself. You do not need to wash yourself clean before you can approach Him. You do not have to long for His touch from a distance, wishing you were good enough or pure enough. Come to Him with all your sins and all your burdens—He will make you clean. The same Jesus who gave His body for your healing also gave His blood for your forgiveness. Just come to Him!

TODAY'S THOUGHT

The Bible does not tell us exactly *what* this woman heard about Jesus, but I submit to you that she must have heard story after story of how Jesus healed the sick everywhere He went. She must have heard how good and gracious He was regardless of how imperfect the ones who came to Him for healing were. The result? Faith ignited in her and the moment she touched the hem of His garment, she received her miracle. What are you hearing about Jesus?

TODAY'S PRAYER

Beloved Lord Jesus, thank You for the truth I am hearing about You and for Your invitation to come just as I am and allow You to make me clean. Because You gave Your body for my healing and Your blood for my forgiveness, I believe I am qualified. Right now, I simply receive my healing and all that I need from You. Amen.

DAY 41

YOU ARE QUALIFIED

Giving thanks to the Father who has qualified us to be partakers of the inheritance of the saints in the light. He has delivered us from the power of darkness and conveyed us into the kingdom of the Son of His love, in whom we have redemption through His blood, the forgiveness of sins.

—Colossians 1:12–14

Years ago, when I first started preaching, one of my spiritual heroes back then had said, "There's nothing wrong with God and nothing wrong with His Word. When you don't receive from God, there's something wrong with you." So that's what I taught my church too. I wanted my people to be healed and whole, and that's why I taught them a list of reasons they were not receiving their healings, but that list just kept growing.

One day, I heard the voice of the Holy Spirit on the inside of me saying, "Stop disqualifying My people!"

I countered, "But Lord, I am not disqualifying them. I am trying to qualify them for Your healing."

As I said that, my eyes were opened, and I repented. I cannot qualify anyone for healing, and neither do I need to try. God has *already* qualified us through the blood of His Son. The Word of God states this so clearly in the verses above.

Today you and I can give thanks to the Father who *has* qualified us. We are *already* qualified to partake of every blessing. And not only that,

He has already *delivered* us from the power of darkness and conveyed us into the kingdom of the Son of His love. That means the devil no longer has any hold over us. He has no power over us. He has no authority to rob us of our health.

Whatever sin you might have committed, whatever mistakes you might have made, stop disqualifying yourself. Maybe you don't think you deserve to be healed because of all the junk food you have eaten for years or because you haven't been exercising. Nothing you can do is so powerful it can wash away the finished work of Christ.

Yes, we should eat healthily and take care of our bodies. But what I am saying is that even if you have made mistakes, you don't have to disqualify yourself. That's what grace is about—*grace is for the undeserving*!

There is nothing wrong with God, nothing wrong with His Word, and definitely nothing wrong with you because Jesus has effectively and perfectly removed all your sins through His blood. He has already qualified you to freely receive His healing. You can boldly declare "Yes" and "Amen" to this promise of God in Christ (2 Cor. 1:20). Now receive your healing!

TODAY'S THOUGHT

When you begin to become more and more conscious of Jesus having been crucified on your behalf, faith no longer is a barrier to receiving God's promises. Why? Because the more you see what Jesus has done for you, the more you see what Jesus has *qualified* you for, the more faith springs up within you, and miracles break forth. Hallelujah!

TODAY'S PRAYER

Lord Jesus, thank You for qualifying me to partake of every blessing and for delivering me from the power of darkness. Thank You for the amazing grace of Your finished work that qualifies me to receive Your healing as well as forgiveness. I declare "Yes" and "Amen" to all the promises and blessings I have in You. Amen.

DAY 42

THE GOODNESS OF GOD

God's kindness leads you to repentance [that is, to change your inner self, your old way of thinking—seek His purpose for your life].

—Romans 2:4 AMP

I want to share with you a testimony that Shirley from Texas sent to my ministry. I pray it will encourage you.

In the natural, there were many things in Shirley's former lifestyle that would have disqualified her from receiving God's healing. For ten years, she was addicted to drugs and alcohol. As a result of that lifestyle, she contracted hepatitis C, a serious and unfortunately silent liver disease, which is chronic and sometimes fatal.

Shirley shared how although the Lord had delivered her from her addictions, she felt she had fallen short as a Christian even when she was trying her best. She kept feeling she wasn't good enough to be healed. But then, in her own words, the "radical grace of God" came into her situation and this is what happened:

I began listening to Joseph Prince and also began to partake of the holy Communion at home and to stand on Jesus' finished work. Sometime later, I went to see an infectious disease specialist to do blood work in order to find out what genotype of hepatitis C I had to get the right treatment. A few weeks later, the doctor called to say she had good news for me: I was a rare individual because I had developed antibodies against the virus and was now immune to it, so I didn't need any treatments. Praise Jesus! All glory to Him! As Jesus is, so am I in this world. As He doesn't have hepatitis C in His blood, neither do I!

What is so neat about this is I felt I had not been spending as much time with God as I would have liked to. I felt like I had fallen short as a Christian. I hadn't even been to church that much. This is a strong message for me—that there is nothing I can do to earn my healing or right standing with the Father. The fact I have felt less spiritual over the past year but was still healed is a powerful testament to the radical grace of our Lord Jesus Christ.

On top of that, I usually get sick at least three to four times during the winter months, but over the last year every time I felt like I was starting to get sick, I would claim Jesus' finished work over my body. I would wake up the next morning healed and refreshed! Praise God!

There were many areas of failure in Shirley's life, yet God in His grace delivered her from ten years of heavy addiction. And as she kept listening to preaching about Jesus, receiving the gift of righteousness, and partaking of the holy Communion, not only did she remain sober but she was also delivered from hepatitis C. Shirley says God's grace "has changed my life." Truly, it is the goodness of God that leads us to repentance.

TODAY'S THOUGHT

Shirley heard the good news that she did not have to have her life all together in order for God to heal her. What you hear about God could mean the difference between life and death. Are you hearing the voice of disqualification or the voice of grace that qualifies you based on the cross of Jesus?

TODAY'S PRAYER

Lord Jesus, thank You for Your amazing grace, Your forgiveness, and Your gift of righteousness that qualifies me to be delivered and healed. Thank You for Your goodness and kindness that have led me to see there is nothing I need to do to earn my healing. I stand on Your finished work and freely receive my healing as I partake of the holy Communion. Amen.

DAY 43

HE IS WILLING

When He had come down from the mountain, great multitudes followed Him. And behold, a leper came and worshiped Him, saying, "Lord, if You are willing, You can make me clean." Then Jesus put out His hand and touched him, saying, "I am willing; be cleansed." Immediately his leprosy was cleansed.

—*Matthew 8:1–3*

You have seen how our Lord Jesus healed the woman with the issue of blood. I want to show you how Jesus healed another person who was also disqualified and considered unclean under the Levitical law. Matthew 8 takes place at the Mount of Beatitudes right after Jesus preached the Sermon on the Mount, and it opens with the verses above.

One of my favorite places to visit in Israel is the Mount of Beatitudes. A number of years ago, I climbed up to where Jesus could have sat while He preached to the multitudes below, then I walked along a path that I realized led all the way to Capernaum. I had always imagined Jesus going down the mountain toward the multitude, but I realized that if He had, it wouldn't say "great multitudes followed Him." Very likely, He had to be walking down another side of the mountain toward Capernaum for the multitudes to follow Him. Just one verse after Jesus healed the man with leprosy, the Bible tells us He entered Capernaum (Matt. 8:5), so that makes sense to me.

As I walked along that path, I came to a huge pile of rocks on the side and noticed other slabs of stone strewn nearby. All of a sudden, I felt the

Lord arrest me, and He began to give me an inner vision. I saw how the man with leprosy could have hidden under those rocks so he could hear Jesus preach without being seen by the multitudes. Had he been seen, being unclean because of his leprosy, people repulsed by his condition might have hurled stones at him to drive him away.

I saw the anguish of the man whose body was covered with leprous sores and raw, exposed flesh, and who had also been forced to isolate himself and be cut off from his loved ones so he would not contaminate or defile them (Lev. 13:45–46). I saw the desperation of the man who threw himself before Jesus, worshiping Him as he said, "Lord, if You are willing, You can make me clean." And I saw the beauty and the majesty of our Lord Jesus as He *touched* the man with leprosy and pronounced, "I am willing; be cleansed."

In that moment, the Lord didn't just restore the man's health, He also restored his humanity.

That Jesus touched a man with leprosy is amazing. Under the law, when the clean touches the unclean, the clean becomes unclean. Our Lord Jesus was showing that under grace, when the clean (Jesus) touches the unclean, the unclean becomes clean! Jesus did not contract defilement by touching the man with leprosy—He banished it. Beloved, He will do the same for you.

TODAY'S THOUGHT

Based on what I saw in the Spirit, I worked with my team to prepare a video of the healing of the man with leprosy so you can experience it too, and I have included the web address here: JosephPrince.com/eat. As you watch it, may you sense the depths of our Lord's compassion and feel His tender love for you. May you see that His holiness is a holiness that can be approached, and may you see Him coming to you, seeking you out, and lifting you out from your pain.

TODAY'S PRAYER

Lord Jesus, thank You for showing me in the Gospels Your great love and power in the way You ministered to the man with leprosy. I believe You are loving me with that same compassion and that You are reaching out to me right now to lift me out of discouragement and sickness. I gladly receive Your tender love and Your healing touch today. Amen.

DAY 44

A GRACE GIFT

In him we have redemption through his blood, the forgiveness of sins, in accordance with the riches of God's grace that he lavished on us.

—Ephesians 1:7–8 NIV

There are many people who believe God has the power to heal. But like the man with leprosy in yesterday's reading, they doubt that God is willing to use His power to heal them. If you have ever entertained such doubts about His willingness to heal you, may it forever be settled in your heart as you hear Jesus say to you, "I am willing, be cleansed! Be healed!" Your sins and shortcomings do not repulse Jesus. On the contrary, the very things you believe disqualify you *qualify* you for His saving grace. As you worship Him and look away from your disqualifications, let Him touch you and make you clean.

Healing is a grace gift. You cannot earn healing by your good works, and neither can your shortcomings cause you to be disqualified from receiving it. Just think about every person whom Jesus healed. Of the great multitudes that were healed, don't you think there were people who had sin and failures in their lives? Did any of those whom Jesus healed have to do anything to earn or qualify for their healing first?

Beloved, stop disqualifying yourself. No matter how you think you have failed, no matter how dirty and unclean you think you are, God loves you. Just as He cleansed the man with leprosy and healed the woman with the issue of blood, He can heal you, and He is most willing.

Under the law, you would be disqualified. But Jesus came to fulfill every jot and every tittle of the law (Matt. 5:17–18) so that today we can freely receive the good we do not deserve. Our Lord Jesus bore our sins as well as our sicknesses on the cross. When God looks at you, He does not see your sins and failures. If you have accepted Jesus into your heart, you are a new creation in Christ (2 Cor. 5:17). Come boldly and receive help for every need (Heb. 4:16)!

I pray that today you have heard about a Jesus who freely releases blessings, provision, and healing with a lavish hand that does not hold back. I pray that you have seen a Jesus who demonstrated His willingness to take your sicknesses and uncleanness and give you His divine health and righteousness in exchange.

TODAY'S THOUGHT

You don't need to earn God's love. In Christ, you are *already* His beloved. All that He has is already yours. He is not asking you to serve Him so you can earn His blessings. All that He has, He has already freely and unconditionally given to you. Come to the Father. Come with all your failings, with all your brokenness, with all your inadequacies. Come as you are and receive from Him all that you need.

TODAY'S PRAYER

Daddy God, thank You that I don't have to qualify for or earn Your gracious gift of healing. Thank You that You love me and care for me. Thank You for Jesus who took all my sins and failures and qualified me for all Your blessings. I receive from Your lavish hand the provision and healing that I need. Amen.

DAY 45

SOMETHING FAR BETTER

"Eye has not seen, nor ear heard, nor have entered into the heart of man the things which God has prepared for those who love Him." But God has revealed them to us through His Spirit.

—1 Corinthians 2:9–10

We have come to the end of this section, but maybe you still have doubts about your healing.

You saw how Jesus healed the woman of a chronic, long-term affliction and cleansed the man of an incurable disease. Perhaps you are thinking, *Yes, but they met Jesus in person. If I could just meet Jesus in person, I could be healed.*

My friend, I have such good news for you.

Our Lord Jesus Himself told His disciples, "It is to your advantage that I go away; for if I do not go away, the Helper will not come to you; but if I depart, I will send Him to you" (John 16:7). When Jesus was on earth, He was limited. He could only be at one place at a time. But now that He has sent us the Holy Spirit, it is to our advantage! He is completely unlimited, and He can say this to you and me:

"I am with you always, even to the end of the age." (Matt. 28:20)

Hallelujah! Jesus is, right now—in the present tense—*with* you and me. He is not far away. Wherever we may be and whatever circumstances we might face, He is with us. Our part is to come *boldly* to Him to receive His mercy, His grace, and His help (Heb. 4:16). Don't disqualify yourself anymore or allow anyone to tell you that you do not deserve His gift of healing. Come boldly to Him today.

And that's not all. Did you notice that the woman with the issue of blood was healed just by touching Jesus' clothes? Today you have something *far* better than His clothes. You get to partake of *Jesus' body* in a tangible and practical way.

What do I mean by this? On the night our Lord Jesus was betrayed, He instituted the holy Communion. He took bread, and the Bible tells us:

> *When He had given thanks, He broke it and said, "Take, eat;* this is My body which is broken for you; *do this in remembrance of Me." In the same manner He also took the cup after supper, saying, "This cup is the new covenant in My blood. This do, as often as you drink it, in remembrance of Me." (1 Cor. 11:24–25)*

Every time we partake of the holy Communion, we are partaking of Jesus' own body and we are receiving His blood. If even His garments contained such healing virtue, can you imagine what power is packed into the holy Communion? There is so much I want to share with you about the healing power of the holy Communion, and I cannot wait to dive further in!

TODAY'S THOUGHT

If touching just Jesus' garments released power for a healing miracle, imagine the power that would be imparted to you if you partook of the Lord's body itself. Imagine partaking of the strength and sickness-repelling life flowing in His body. That is the opportunity and blessing available to us whenever we receive the Communion. The more you allow the Holy Spirit to unveil just how beautiful Jesus is in the holy Communion, the more His healing virtue will explode in your body.

TODAY'S PRAYER

Father in heaven, thank You that the Holy Spirit has come to live in me and is revealing to me all that I have through Jesus' finished work. Thank You that Jesus is always with me and is present in a tangible and practical way through the holy Communion. As I partake of the Communion today, I believe I am receiving a fresh impartation of His healing power and divine life in every part of my body. Amen.

TESTIMONY

Vision Completely Restored After Receiving Communion

Several years ago, after moving to west Texas for work, I began to experience problems with my vision. It became blurry and in a matter of days, I could not even see the images on a fifty-two-inch television screen or read the texts on my cell phone.

I was taken to an ophthalmologist who said my case was severe and suggested that I see an eye specialist. The specialist who diagnosed my eye condition told me that both my retinas had detached. I had to get immediate treatment or I could become totally blind. He also told my family that because I did not have health insurance, doctors would not want to see me.

My mom and I committed the situation to the Lord, believing He would open the doors we needed. Long story short, by His grace, I was able to see the best physicians. I went for eye tests that showed both my retinas had detached and that I was officially blind. They told me I might not ever get my vision back. One doctor stated he had seen this condition before in very elderly people but not in a thirty-five-year-old like me. They wrote on my report that not only were my retinas detached, but everything behind my eyes was also out of order. Nothing was where it was supposed to be and they had no explanation as to how or why this had happened.

I got depressed because I could not drive and needed help to climb the stairs or step off a curb. It was better for my eyes if I sat in a dark room to avoid all the light, but this made me even more depressed. It was a very challenging time, and I often thought about dying.

I was prescribed several types of medication, some of which made me gain weight. The doctors told me I might have to remain on medication for the rest of my life and that I should not drive or work until my vision improved. I did not want to be on medication for life, not to mention the costs involved. On my own, I stopped taking the medications and didn't tell my doctors about it.

Even though my retinas remained detached, we kept believing and thanking the Lord for my healing. We had been listening to Joseph Prince, and I kept declaring, "As Jesus is so am I in this world." We also prayed whenever we visited the doctor, believing for a good report.

One morning, my mom proposed that we partake of the holy Communion prior to heading for my medical appointment. She had been hearing Joseph Prince for some time now and had learned more about the holy Communion and what it means. We partook of the Communion in faith and thanked the Lord for a good report that morning.

WE PARTOOK OF THE COMMUNION IN FAITH AND THANKED THE LORD FOR A GOOD REPORT. . . . THAT MORNING, I SAW HOW GRACE HEALED ME.

At the doctor's clinic, the normal routine test was performed. After that, the doctor looked in my eyes and declared my retinas were no longer detached and that everything behind my eyes was back in place. She muttered, "Unbelievable," under her breath and said, "You never would have known this patient had retinal detachment." She added that she had never seen such a quick recovery and called in two other doctors so they could confirm and witness what she was seeing.

My entire ordeal lasted about ten months but that morning I saw how grace healed me. My vision has been completely restored. I can now see the texts on my cell phone, the images on TV, and I am also working and driving. Glory to Jesus!

Albert | Texas, United States

SECTION VII

REVELATION BRINGS RESULTS

That the God of our Lord Jesus Christ, the Father of glory, may give to you the spirit of wisdom and revelation in the knowledge of Him, the eyes of your understanding being enlightened; that you may know what is the hope of His calling, what are the riches of the glory of His inheritance in the saints, and what is the exceeding greatness of His power toward us who believe, according to the working of His mighty power which He worked in Christ when He raised Him from the dead and seated Him at His right hand in the heavenly places.

—Ephesians 1:17–20

DAY 46

NOT ABOUT RULES AND RITUALS

Do you not know that your body is the temple of the Holy Spirit who is in you, whom you have from God, and you are not your own? For you were bought at a price.

—1 Corinthians 6:19–20

If you have been reading this book from the start, I pray you have begun to see that *whatever* medical condition you or your loved one might have, there is hope.

There is hope because you are *not* on your own, and you are *not your own*—you belong to a God who loves you with an incomprehensible love, a love that surpasses knowledge, a love that is too great and intense to ever understand (Eph. 3:18–19).

There is hope because you belong to a God who could not leave you to suffer disease and sickness and sent His own beloved Son to bear *all* your pains and your sicknesses upon His own body.

There is hope because you belong to a God who has given you a practical way by which you can have access to His healing power *any time*. You can come to Him freely. There are no religious hoops to jump through, no qualifications you have to meet. He has *already* qualified you, and the only thing you need to do is to respond to His invitation when He took the bread and said, "*Take, eat*; this is My body," when He took the cup and said, "*Drink from it*, all of you" (Matt. 26:26–27).

I pray that you have caught a revelation of *what* to eat to live a life that is brimming with vitality and have a body that is filled with divine health and strength. In this and the next chapter, I want to share with you about *how* to eat of the Lord's Supper for life and health, which is completely different from any other diet you may have tried.

Every diet and eating plan has its own set of rules—dos and don'ts—you need to adhere to in order to see results and breakthroughs. You have to follow through on all the tenets of the diet or there will be minimal or no results. The point is, the results of any diet are entirely dependent on you—on *your* discipline, *your* willpower, and *your* ability to maintain and keep the rules.

When it comes to the holy Communion, the results have nothing to do with what you need to do, and everything to do with having a revelation of what was done *for you*. Whenever you read the Bible, remember it's not just a historical text or a record of the life of our Lord Jesus. The Bible documents His love *for you*! I pray that the Holy Spirit has given you eyes to see that all Jesus endured was *for you*. *You* and your wholeness were the joy that was set before Him. Every sacrifice He made was *for you*. The divine One suffered *for you* to have divine life, health, and wholeness!

TODAY'S THOUGHT

Remember, the holy Communion is not about examining yourself for sins committed and determining what you need to do to make yourself worthy to partake. My friend, it is all about looking to Jesus and seeing what He has accomplished on the cross to make you worthy to partake and to give you healing and an abundance of health.

TODAY'S PRAYER

Father God, thank You that I belong to You because the precious blood and body of Your beloved Son were given for me. Thank You that You sent Jesus to bear my pains and sicknesses on His body. As I partake of the holy Communion, I ask for the Holy Spirit to open my eyes to see all that Jesus has done for me and help me to receive the wholeness He has purchased for me. Amen.

DAY 47

PARTAKING IN REMEMBRANCE

[He] took bread; and when He had given thanks, He broke it and said, "Take, eat; this is My body which is broken for you; do this in remembrance of Me." In the same manner He also took the cup after supper, saying, "This cup is the new covenant in My blood. This do, as often as you drink it, in remembrance of Me."

—1 Corinthians 11:23–25

The results for diets and exercise come from rules, routine, and regimentation. The results from the holy Communion come from relationship, revelation, and understanding the redemptive work of Christ. The Communion is about His love. It is about His power to heal you and deliver you from every sickness and disease. And that is why the apostle Paul wrote in the verses above that our Lord Jesus wants us to partake of the holy Communion in *remembrance* of Him.

When the Jewish people use the word *remembrance*, it is a much stronger word than just a passive or sentimental remembering. It has the idea of *reenactment*, of going through the event again. It is about reenacting all Jesus went through, seeing His body broken as you break the bread in your hands, and seeing His blood being shed for you as you drink of the cup. It is about actively valuing the cross, and seeing how powerful it is for you today as you remember it was for you that the King of kings suffered.

Did you notice that our Lord Jesus told us to partake of the holy Communion in *remembrance of Him* and not in remembrance of our medical conditions? There was a time when many of the children of Israel were dying from snakebites in the wilderness. When Moses prayed that the Lord would take the serpents away, He responded, "Make a fiery serpent, and set it on a pole; and it shall be that everyone who is bitten, when he looks at it, shall live" (Num. 21:8).

God did not take away the serpents. His response was to instruct Moses to make a replica of the very thing that was killing them—the serpent—and to set it on a pole for all to look at. "So Moses made a bronze serpent, and put it on a pole; and so it was, if a serpent had bitten anyone, when he looked at the bronze serpent, he lived" (Num. 21:9).

The serpent on the pole is a picture of our Lord Jesus being lifted up on the cross, suspended between heaven and earth, rejected by man and also by His own Father because He was carrying all our sins. On that cross He bore every consequence and every curse of sin that you and I should have experienced, and that includes every sickness and every disease.

Today, whatever your condition, come to the Lord's Table. Come, beholding Him and His love and begin to partake more and more of the healing that He paid for you to have.

TODAY'S THOUGHT

God instructed Moses to make a bronze serpent because bronze in the Bible speaks of judgment. God is holy and just, and God has to punish sin. God loved you and me so much that He sent Jesus to be our substitute, to bear our punishment for every sin. Your sins have been judged and your sicknesses borne in His own body. All you need to do on your part is to look to Jesus and believe He has done it all for you to be healed.

TODAY'S PRAYER

Precious Lord Jesus, thank You for Your amazing love for me. Every time I partake of the holy Communion, help me to take my eyes off my symptoms and pain and remember anew what You went through for me to secure my healing. I lift the eyes of my heart to see all that You did for me at the cross, and I rest in Your perfect finished work to heal me from every sickness. Amen.

DAY 48

LOOK INTENTLY

"And as Moses lifted up the serpent in the wilderness, even so must the Son of Man be lifted up, that whoever believes in Him should not perish but have eternal life."

—John 3:14–15

I want to show you something powerful in the story of Moses lifting up the bronze serpent in the wilderness when the children of Israel were bitten by snakes. I believe it is going to release you to partake of the holy Communion with greater revelation each time you come to the Lord's Table.

In the Numbers 21 account of this story, we read that even though many were killed by the snakebites, anyone among the children of Israel who *looked* at the bronze serpent *was healed*. The Hebrew word used for *look* in Numbers 21:9 is *nabat*, which means to "look intently at."[1] In the same way, when you partake of the holy Communion, be conscious of Jesus and how He bore all your sins and sicknesses in His own body. Don't partake with consciousness of the symptoms in your body.

Beloved, I know that the waves of nausea that immobilize you are real. The shortness of breath you have been struggling with is real. The pain that slices through your head with every move is real, just as the painful bites from the fiery serpents were real for the children of Israel. Right now, I pray that every pain and every discomfort be removed from your body in the mighty name of Jesus. Our Lord Jesus called healing "the children's bread" (Matt. 15:26). If you are a child of God, healing belongs to you.

But my friend, your healing will not come from focusing on your condition. Your healing will come as you do what the children of Israel did—they looked away from their wounds and looked at the bronze serpent lifted up on the pole. Today, as you partake of the Communion, partake in remembrance of your Lord Jesus and not in remembrance of your pain. Look to Him intently and with the expectation He will save you and heal you.

See Him lifted on the cross, being judged with your disease. If you have a problem with your kidney, see Jesus' kidney smitten with your disease at the cross. If you have a degenerative condition in your spine, see Jesus' spine smitten with that condition at the cross. When you see Jesus' body smitten with your disease, it cannot remain in you. Even if you have a "terminal" disease others have died from, look to Him and receive your healing!

TODAY'S THOUGHT

Whenever you partake of the holy Communion, may I encourage you not to rush through it? The Lord loves you so much. Take some time to worship Him until you can sense His presence. Take time to magnify Him until your consciousness of His goodness and His healing virtue is so much greater than the feelings of your infirmity or the symptoms in your loved one's body. As you worship the person of our Lord Jesus, I believe you will receive all the benefits of the work that come with the person. That's why we partake in remembrance of Him.

TODAY'S PRAYER

Lord Jesus, thank You for how the bronze serpent shows me that I have been delivered from every sickness and curse because You were judged in my place at the cross. I can never praise You enough for becoming cursed in my place because of my sins. I believe that as I keep looking intently to You, my wonderful Savior, I will receive my healing. Amen.

DAY 49

SET APART FOR LIFE AND HEALTH

But you are a chosen people, a royal priesthood, a holy nation, God's special possession, that you may declare the praises of him who called you out of darkness into his wonderful light.

—1 Peter 2:9 NIV

Some people are thrown off by the word *holy* when we talk about the holy Communion. To them, it feels antiquated and maybe even irrelevant. But did you know that to be "holy" simply means to be "set apart for God"[1] and to be *uncommon*? This speaks of the special nature of the Communion. Every time you partake of the holy Communion, you are allowing the Lord to set you apart from the world, and allowing Him to have a private time of intimacy and communion with you! Look at what God did for the children of Israel when the plagues came upon the land of Egypt. He declared:

> *"And in that day I will set apart the land of Goshen, in which My people dwell, that no swarms of flies shall be there, in order that you may know that I am the* Lord *in the midst of the land. I will make a difference between My people and your people."* (Ex. 8:22–23)

In the same way, when you have divine insights on the power and significance of the holy Communion, the Lord Himself sets you apart and makes a difference between you and the people of the world. That means you are *not* like the people of the world. That means it may be common for the people of the world to catch the "common flu," or common for people in a particular age demographic to experience certain symptoms or to develop certain conditions. But you don't have to accept any "common" ailments because God has set you apart to be uncommon.

In a world that is decaying and dying of illness, He has paid the price for you to be uncommonly healthy, whole, and healed. While the rest of the world can weaken with age, the Bible declares that "as your days, so shall your strength be" (Deut. 33:25), and that even as you advance in age, you can return to the days of your youth (Job 33:25). I pray that over you right now: as your days increase, may your strength and your health also increase, and may the Lord return the days of your youth to you, and cause your flesh to be young like a child's. Amen!

TODAY'S THOUGHT

In the land of Goshen, God's people were protected from the ten plagues that besieged the land of Egypt during the time of Moses. God makes a distinction between His people and the people of the world. We are *in* this world, but we are not *of* this world (John 17:14). We are His. We, who have been drawn near to God through the work of His Son, can have intimacy with Him and enjoy His protective covering to live full of health.

TODAY'S PRAYER

Father, thank You for setting me apart from the world to reflect Your glory upon my life. Thank You that no matter what happens in the world, I can live fear-free and uncommonly healthy because Jesus has paid the price. I draw near to You and receive Your strength, renewal, and healing. In Jesus' name, amen.

DAY 50

REVELATION AND RELATIONSHIP

My child, pay attention to what I say.
Listen carefully to my words.
Don't lose sight of them.
Let them penetrate deep into your heart,
for they bring life to those who find them,
and healing to their whole body.

—*Proverbs 4:20–22* NLT

There is something about the holy Communion that you must know: simply ingesting the elements of the holy Communion will not yield results.

When I first started teaching our church about the Communion, some of my church members would simply tell their friends who fell sick to partake of the Communion. While I understood their intentions, just going through the motions of eating the bread and drinking the cup devoid of a *relationship* with our loving Savior does not work.

You can't just eat the elements out of superstition or with the attitude of simply "trying it out." You can't just put Communion elements in the hands of your loved ones who are sick and simply tell them to eat. As I mentioned before, there is nothing magical about the elements of the Communion. If you have no revelation of the significance of the Communion, and no sense of the love of the Lord Jesus in your heart, the holy Communion becomes empty. Unlike diets and fitness plans, which work if you follow the prescribed rules, the power of the holy Communion is based on a *revelation* of the redemptive work of Christ and faith in His finished work.

If you don't have a revelation or you don't have faith, start listening to and watching sermons that are full of Jesus. Listen to teachings or read books about the holy Communion that unveil what He has done for you. The Bible tells us "faith comes by hearing, and hearing by the word of God" (Rom. 10:17). Did you notice that it doesn't say faith comes by "having heard"? If you don't have faith, you can cause faith to "come" by hearing and hearing. So keep on hearing, and don't be satisfied with simply having heard.

The New International Version translation of this verse also explains that faith comes by hearing "the word about Christ." Faith does not come by hearing about what you need to do to earn your blessing or how you have failed. It comes by hearing all about *Jesus* and His overwhelming love for you.

TODAY'S THOUGHT

Beloved, hearing plays a huge part in revelation. Faith comes by hearing teachings that have been filtered through Jesus' finished work and the new covenant of grace. The more you hear Jesus unveiled, expounded upon, and pointed to in the Scriptures, the more faith will be imparted to your heart to understand everything God's Word says about you so you can receive your healing from your loving Savior.

TODAY'S PRAYER

Father, I ask You to reveal more and more of Jesus and His love as I keep hearing and reading the Word about Christ. I thank You that I don't have to worry about not having faith because it will come as I see and hear more of the beauty, grace, and goodness of Jesus unveiled in Your Word. Thank You that as I focus on Jesus, faith and Your healing power are being imparted to me. Amen.

DAY 51
INTIMATE FELLOWSHIP

But the one who is united and joined to the Lord is one spirit with Him.

—1 Corinthians 6:17 AMP

Let me share with you something that I pray will cause your heart to be filled with such warmth as you see more and more of Jesus. The very word *communion* speaks of the relationship our Lord desires to have with us. The apostle Paul wrote:

> *The cup of blessing which we bless, is it not the communion of the blood of Christ? The bread which we break, is it not the communion of the body of Christ? For we, though many, are one bread and one body; for we all partake of that one bread. Observe Israel after the flesh: Are not those who eat of the sacrifices partakers of the altar? (1 Cor. 10:16–18)*

The word used for *communion* in the original Greek is the word *koinonia*, meaning "fellowship."[1] It also has the idea of an intimate participation, like the intimacy a husband and wife share when they say and do things no one else is privy to. Isn't that beautiful? Whenever you partake of the Communion, it's a time of intimacy between you and the Lord. It's a time you set aside to remember your heavenly Bridegroom, who loved you so much He gave Himself up for you (Eph. 5:25). It's a time you run to Him and lose yourself in His presence, and let His perfect love cast out every fear that may be eating at you.

He knows the secret fears of your heart as you look at the symptoms in your body. He knows the burdens that weigh you down as the doctors tell you about the long-term complications, side effects, and financial cost that treatment would entail. Run to Him, and cast all your anxieties, all your worries, and all your concerns on Him, for He cares about you with deepest affection and watches over you very carefully (1 Peter 5:7 AMP).

As you take time to commune with Him and to remember Him through the holy Communion, do you know what happens? You become an intimate participator of the benefits of the body and the blood. Just as those who ate of the sacrifices become "partakers of the altar" (1 Cor. 10:18), when you eat the bread and drink the cup, you become a partaker of all Jesus accomplished at the cross. As you drink the cup, that is communion with and sharing in the blood of Christ (1 Cor. 10:16 NASB). As you eat of the broken bread, you are participating in the body of Christ that was broken for you (1 Cor. 10:16 NIV).

TODAY'S THOUGHT

Insecurity and love cannot coexist in the truly intimate relationship that God wants with His children. If you are feeling separated from God today, you won't be able to believe Him for His healing grace. May I tell you that in the holy Communion, Jesus invites you to discover, taste, and experience His unconditional love and overcoming power? Will you do that today? Your life will never be the same again.

TODAY'S PRAYER

Beloved Lord Jesus, thank You for inviting me to experience Your perfect love and healing and wholeness when I partake of the holy Communion. I run to You, my heavenly Bridegroom, and cast all my cares on You. As I partake of the Communion today remembering You and Your finished work, I thank You that Your healing and provision are flowing into my body and life. Amen.

DAY 52

EATING FRESH

Therefore, brethren, having boldness to enter the Holiest by the blood of Jesus, by a new and living way which He consecrated for us, through the veil, that is, His flesh.

—Hebrews 10:19–20

When God provided manna for the children of Israel in the wilderness, Moses told the people, "Let no one leave any of it till morning" (Ex. 16:19). When some of them did not heed Moses' words and kept some till the next morning, it bred worms and stank. This reminds me of the law that the children of Israel had to observe when they brought the peace offering for thanksgiving: "The flesh of the sacrifice of his peace offering for thanksgiving shall be eaten the same day it is offered. *He shall not leave any of it until morning*" (Lev. 7:15).

These two verses speak of partaking fresh and not leaving the manna or the meat from the sacrifice to turn stale. In the same way, whenever we partake of the holy Communion, let's ask the Lord for a fresh revelation of what He did for us at the cross. Let's not ever become so familiar with the holy Communion that we start to see it as common and ordinary. We are holding the broken body of the Son of God and drinking of His shed blood.

Would you like to have a fresh revelation of the holy Communion? In today's Scripture passage, God's Word tells us that through the cross, our Lord Jesus consecrated a "new and living way" for us to draw near to God not with fear and trepidation but with *boldness.* He allowed His own flesh to be torn so that we can have free access to our loving Father today. I want to draw your attention to the original Greek word used for *new* here. It is the word *prosphatos*, and it means "lately slaughtered, freshly killed."[1]

Why did the Holy Spirit use this unusual word here? Because whenever you partake of the holy Communion, God does not want you to partake as though you are commemorating a historical event that took place long ago. The cross transcends time. As you partake of the holy Communion in remembrance of Him, see your Lord Jesus before you, as though you are right there at Calvary. See your Lord Jesus *freshly slain*, bearing all your sicknesses and carrying all your pains. Don't partake ritualistically, but press in for a fresh revelation of His love that was demonstrated at the cross.

TODAY'S THOUGHT

I love it when God opens our eyes to see Jesus afresh. He doesn't want us to live on past revelations of Jesus, for His mercies are new every morning (Lam. 3:23). The more revelation you get of His finished work, the more you will receive an impartation of faith for any need, even the seemingly impossible ones. Hallelujah!

TODAY'S PRAYER

Father God, thank You for the new and living way that the Lord Jesus opened for me to draw near to You with boldness. As I partake of the holy Communion, help me to see Him freshly slain, bearing all my sicknesses and carrying all my pains. I believe the power of the cross transcends time, and You are causing the benefits of the cross—healing, restoration, favor, and supply—to flow into my life right now. Amen.

DAY 53
DAILY HEALING

Looking unto Jesus, the author and finisher of our faith, who for the joy that was set before Him endured the cross, despising the shame, and has sat down at the right hand of the throne of God.

—Hebrews 12:2

Let me share with you the powerful testimony of Carey from Kentucky. She wrote about how the Lord showed her that His provision of her healing was fresh every day:

I left an abusive marriage of twelve years, and my kids live with my ex-husband. I am only able to see them twice a year because I live twelve hours away. After my last visit to see my kids, I fell into a deep depression. I couldn't get out of bed and slept up to twenty hours a day. Medications didn't help me. I lost fifty-eight pounds in five months because I couldn't eat.

Pastor Prince, I have been listening to your sermons on the holy Communion, literally for twenty-four hours on some days. I let them play as I sleep and listen for the few hours I am awake. The revelation I received on the Communion has helped me step out of such deep darkness and depression. Like the new manna that fell for the children of Israel every day, God showed me that His daily bread was my daily healing—not for yesterday or tomorrow, but today.

God told me it is the same with the Communion. That today He supplies all my healing through the elements of bread and juice, the simple things that represent what His Son did for me on the cross. When tomorrow comes, He will provide me with new bread and new healing for that day. So I began to take the Communion every day, and especially when I had really dark moments.

And here I stand, depression-free. God has restored hope in my life. Understanding the Communion better has given me hope and showed me that without Jesus hope is just an empty word. All praise to God for His revelation!

Don't you love Jesus? Don't you find such assurance in knowing that your health and healing are based on an intimate relationship with a living Savior? Don't you feel firmly established, knowing that He has done everything for you and your part is to simply look to Him daily and receive His finished work through the holy Communion? I have so much more I want to share with you that I know will bless you and fill your heart with faith to receive from Him.

TODAY'S THOUGHT

May I encourage you not to rush through this book? Don't walk away only having more head knowledge about the holy Communion. My prayer is that you will catch a revelation of Jesus that will cause your heart to burn within you (Luke 24:32). Pause, and take time to worship the King of kings and the Lord of lords. Take time to sing to Him in psalms, hymns, and spiritual songs (Eph. 5:18–19). As you worship Him, He will release His fresh power over you to heal you, deliver you, and bring you the victory. Hallelujah!

TODAY'S PRAYER

Lord Jesus, thank You for the deep assurance that my health and healing are based on my relationship with You. Thank You that I can fix my eyes on You through the holy Communion and return again and again to what You did for me at the cross. I rest in Your finished work, and I believe you are releasing fresh power into my body and over my circumstances to heal, deliver, and bring me the victory. Amen.

SECTION VIII

COMPLETELY COVERED, NO EXCLUSIONS

Grace and peace be multiplied to you in the knowledge of God and of Jesus our Lord, as His divine power has given to us all things that pertain to life and godliness, through the knowledge of Him who called us by glory and virtue, by which have been given to us exceedingly great and precious promises, that through these you may be partakers of the divine nature, having escaped the corruption that is in the world through lust.

—2 Peter 1:2–4

DAY 54

EVERY CONDITION IN EVERY PART

"Then they shall eat the flesh on that night; roasted in fire, with unleavened bread and with bitter herbs they shall eat it. Do not eat it raw, nor boiled at all with water, but roasted in fire—its head with its legs and its entrails."

—Exodus 12:8–9

Thank you for staying with me all this way and giving me the privilege of sharing with you about a God who loves you so much He gave up His own Son to pay the price for your healing. But maybe you have been wondering if there are exclusions and conditions to God's healing power through the holy Communion. I want to give you the assurance that there are *no exclusions* whatsoever in the finished work of Christ. Its coverage is all-encompassing and perfectly comprehensive, and *every* condition has been covered!

Earlier, I showed you God's instructions on how to partake of the Passover lamb, and in the verses above, I want to highlight another powerful truth. Why did God specifically mention that the lamb should be roasted in fire with its head, legs, and entrails? I believe He wants you to see that Jesus, your Passover Lamb, bore *every* condition in *every* part of your body. There is *no* disease, injury, or sickness He did not carry in His own body on the cross.

The Israelites had lived under the stressful, cruel oppression of their slave masters and the horror of infanticide. Perhaps some of them suffered from post-traumatic stress disorder or had recurrent panic attacks.

Perhaps some had chronic pain and physical disabilities from being brutally treated by their slave masters. But whatever condition they might have suffered from, I believe they were healed as they ate the roasted head, legs, and entrails of the lamb.

Whatever affliction you might have in any part of your body, I want you to know every condition has been borne by Jesus on the cross. While God specifically instructed the children of Israel to eat the Passover lamb's head with its legs and entrails, the *whole* lamb was roasted. This means no matter what disease you are battling today, Jesus has taken it on Himself.

Your part is to keep partaking of the channel of divine health He has given you until you see the manifestation of your victory. Your part is to lift up your hands to Him and say, "Lord Jesus, I receive Your healing. By the stripes that fell on You, every part of my body—every cell, every organ—is healed and functions at peak efficiency. Thank You, Jesus, for Your healing."

TODAY'S THOUGHT

Even if you have received a discouraging medical report and your chances of recovery are very slim in the natural, God can heal you. Don't give up. Keep believing. Whatever medical science or doctors have said, the name of Jesus is higher and more powerful than any disease or sickness. Nothing is too hard for the Lord (Jer. 32:27).

TODAY'S PRAYER

Lord Jesus, thank You that You are the Passover Lamb of God who took away my sin and bore every condition in every part of my body on the cross. Thank You that there is no disease, injury, or sickness that is not covered by Your finished work. I believe that nothing is too hard for You. I rest in You, and I receive my healing now. Amen.

DAY 55

FULLY RESTORED

He refreshes and restores my soul (life).

—Psalm 23:3 AMP

Jesus, our Passover Lamb, took upon Himself any condition that affects any part of your body and wants you healed of it. I want you to meditate on how He bore these infirmities so you can have perfect freedom from them (Matt. 8:17). For instance, if you or a loved one has a neurological condition such as recurrent migraines, encephalitis, meningitis, dementia, or are suffering the effects of a stroke, see your Savior's brain afflicted with the condition on the cross as you partake of the Lord's Supper.

Let me share with you a powerful testimony of healing from Alzheimer's disease that Paula from Texas sent to me:

My mother was ravaged by Alzheimer's disease. She was debilitated to the point that she did not recognize her family members. My parents live with me so I could see the daily moment-to-moment struggles and hardship. It was a miserable existence for her as well as for those of us trying to care for her. There were times I just missed my mom and wished to see her well again.

Then one day, my sister shared a praise report with me after following your teaching on the holy Communion, so I immediately began to partake of the Communion with my mother. My mother went to bed on the third night after receiving the Communion and woke up the next day looking ten years younger. All the things she had forgotten how to do, she is doing again. She remembers who we all are now. She has stopped repeating herself, something she used to do from sun up to sun down, and is a complete joy to be around now. Jesus has healed her mind and set her free!

We are still rejoicing that she is back. I asked her about her experience and the best she could describe was that she was lost and trapped, but that's all over now. Nothing is too big for the finished work of Christ Jesus, and I praise Him for it. It has freed my mother!

To God be all the glory and all the praise! As you advance in years, don't accept the lie that you will become more forgetful. When the psalmist wrote that God "restores my soul," he used the word *nephesh* for *soul*. *Nephesh* includes your life, your emotions, and also your mind.[1] Even if you have experienced some degeneration in this area, the Lord can restore. And when the Lord restores, His restoration is always greater than the original in quality!

TODAY'S THOUGHT

The world says that as your days increase and you age, your strength diminishes. But the Word declares, "As your days, so shall your strength be" (Deut. 33:25). Whose report will you believe? Keep partaking of the Lord's Supper and see yourself partaking of the mind of Christ. I declare that your mind is getting healthier and healthier in Jesus' name!

TODAY'S PRAYER

Heavenly Father, thank You that there is no disease or condition that is too big for the finished work of Your Son. Thank

You that each time I come to you, You are restoring my body, my emotions, and my mind. I will keep partaking of the holy Communion and declaring that my body and mind are getting healthier and healthier. As my days, so shall my strength be. In Jesus' name, amen.

DAY 56

LOOSED FROM YOUR CHAINS

"Cursed is the ground because of you; through painful toil you will eat food from it all the days of your life. It will produce thorns and thistles for you, and you will eat the plants of the field. By the sweat of your brow you will eat your food."

—Genesis 3:17–19 NIV

Before Jesus went through the scourging for our diseases, the Bible tells us He was under such duress in the Garden of Gethsemane that "His sweat became like great drops of blood falling down to the ground" (Luke 22:44). I believe that Jesus experienced a rare medical condition called "hematidrosis," where a person under extreme stress actually sweats blood.[1]

This is significant because of what happened in another garden, the garden of Eden. The verses above tell us that God said the ground was cursed with thorns because of Adam's sin, resulting in Adam having to toil and sweat to get it to produce food. In other words, work became stressful. But when Jesus' sweat mingled with His redeeming blood, He delivered us from the curse of stress.

Thorns are also a picture of the cares of this world. When Jesus explained the parable of the sower, He referred to the thorns as the "cares of this world and the deceitfulness of riches" (Matt. 13:22). No wonder Jesus allowed the crown of thorns to be rammed onto His head. The next time you partake of the holy Communion, don't rush through it. See your Lord Jesus pierced not just by the nails but also by the thorns.

It was all for you. It was all for your freedom. The children of Israel were set free from physical chains and shackles. Today I declare to you in Jesus' name that you are loosed from the chains of stress and any stress-induced condition. Stress can cause cardiovascular diseases, eating disorders, menstrual issues, sexual dysfunctions, gastrointestinal problems, as well as skin and hair problems.

And beyond that, remember that the Passover lamb's head, legs, and entrails were to be eaten. That means *any* condition of your eyes, nose, throat, ears, and mouth was borne for your healing. It includes *any* affliction that causes you to be weak in your legs or affects your mobility. And it covers *all* your internal organs (what "entrails" speak of), and that includes your stomach, bowels, heart, kidneys, liver, prostate, and reproductive organs.

My friend, *whatever* your condition, however long it has kept you bound—two years, ten years, thirty years—I want you to know and believe that God can set you free from it. I speak health, healing, longevity, and wholeness to you in Jesus' mighty name. Amen and amen!

TODAY'S THOUGHT

If you are facing challenges in *any* part of your body today, Jesus has redeemed you completely. As you partake of the Lord's Supper, see Him on the cross smitten with your specific condition and receive His perfect health in that area. May you walk in the fullness of all He died to give you.

TODAY'S PRAYER

Beloved Lord Jesus, thank You that Your redeeming blood has delivered me from the curse of stress and *all* its induced conditions. It has redeemed me from *every* affliction. As I partake of the Communion today, I see You on the cross smitten for my healing, and I receive Your perfect health. Amen.

DAY 57

REDEEMED FROM EVERY CURSE

> *Christ has redeemed us from the curse of the law, having become a curse for us (for it is written, "Cursed is everyone who hangs on a tree"), that the blessing of Abraham might come upon the Gentiles in Christ Jesus, that we might receive the promise of the Spirit through faith.*
>
> —*Galatians 3:13–14*

I pray that you have caught a glimpse of the absolute perfection of Jesus' finished work on the cross, and how much He loves you to have borne every imaginable disease upon His own body so you need *not* suffer them. But I am not done showing you how you can turn to the cross for *any* and *every* medical challenge and condition. The verses above tell us that our Lord Jesus redeemed us from *every* curse of the law so that the blessing of Abraham might come upon us.

Deuteronomy 28 has a long and detailed list of curses, and I want to focus on the curses that cover sicknesses and diseases that Jesus has redeemed you and me from:

- Consumption (diseases that cause your lungs to waste away), fever, and inflammation (Deut. 28:22)
- Boils, tumors, scurvy, "the itch, from which you cannot be cured" (Deut. 28:27 NLT)

- Madness, blindness, and panic (Deut. 28:28 NLT)
- Severe boils that cannot be healed (Deut. 28:35)
- Great and prolonged plagues, and serious and prolonged sicknesses (Deut. 28:59)

Christ has redeemed you from *every single one* of the diseases and afflictions mentioned here. If you think your particular condition is not quite covered, the Bible goes on to mention "all the diseases of Egypt" (Deut. 28:60). Egypt is a picture of the world. As the people of God, we do not have to be afraid of the diseases the world suffers because He has brought us out of the world, and now we may be *in* the world but we are not *of* this world (John 17:11, 14).

Not only that. It also goes on to include "every sickness and every plague, which is not written in this Book of the Law" (Deut. 28:61).

Hallelujah! Can you see that *every* disease and *every* condition is part of the curse of the law and that Christ has redeemed us from *every* curse? God wants you so blessed in your health that just as He put all your sins on Jesus' body, He also put all your diseases on Jesus' body. God loves you so much He allowed His own Son to *become a curse* so you can be redeemed from the curse of the law.

That doesn't mean the enemy won't try to enforce symptoms of the curse in your life. But whenever the enemy tries to bring on a symptom of the curse, you can reject it. Refuse to accept it. You have already been redeemed from that symptom in Jesus' name!

TODAY'S THOUGHT

Aren't you glad Christ has redeemed you from the curse of the law? There is no more judgment, punishment, and curse of sickness for you because the full judgment, punishment, and curse for all your sins fell upon our Lord Jesus at the cross. He has paid it all.

TODAY'S PRAYER

Father God, thank You that Your eternal Word states that every curse and stroke of punishment for my sins was placed upon Jesus' body on the cross. Thank You that He has redeemed us from every single disease that afflicts the world. I reject any symptom of the curse in Jesus' name and believe that by His stripes I am healed. Amen.

DAY 58

HE CAN MAKE A WAY

And Moses said to the people, "Do not be afraid. Stand still, and see the salvation of the LORD, which He will accomplish for you today. For the Egyptians whom you see today, you shall see again no more forever. The LORD will fight for you, and you shall hold your peace."

—Exodus 14:13–14

I may not understand fully the circumstances you are going through today or the depths of your despair as you watch your loved one fighting to stay alive. But what I do know is this: God loves *you* more than you can ever comprehend, and He *can* make a way even when there seems to be no way.

Exodus 14 records how the children of Israel thought they were doomed when the mighty Egyptian army closed in on them. It appeared they would either be slaughtered by the Egyptians or perish in the watery grave of the Red Sea. But read what Moses said to them in the verses above. Then God split open the sea, and the children of Israel "walked on dry land in the midst of the sea" (Ex. 14:29). But God didn't stop there. He caused the sea to return to its full depth while Pharaoh's formidable forces were still in pursuit, and I love how the Bible spells this out: "Not so much as one of them remained" (Ex. 14:28).

Beloved, you or your loved one might be faced with a daunting and seemingly impossible medical situation. All your fretting and tears cannot change your situation, but there is One who can. Do not be afraid.

Stand still and see the salvation of the Lord. *He* will fight for you. *He* will overcome your enemies for you. Don't keep asking *why* you have the disease. Don't accept the disease or believe the lie that you deserve to be sick because of the wrong you have done. The Lord Jesus has *already* paid the price for your wholeness. Just put your hand in His and let Him lead you through your situation.

He will cause you to walk on dry land in the midst of the sea. The negative reports, medical statistics, and symptoms that you see may spell an inescapable situation, but He will make a way that will stun everyone around you. The Red Sea you thought would drown you will become the burial ground for your enemies instead. You might see them today, but you shall see those oppressive symptoms *no more forever*!

I see your migraine headaches gone. The inflammation in your joints gone. The paralyzing fatigue gone. The negative report about your unborn baby gone. The blood in your urine gone. Not so much as one of them will remain!

TODAY'S THOUGHT

Even when experts have tried everything they know and say that you have only months or even days to live, God can make a way. In the face of death, lift up the bread and declare that with every stripe that tore into our Lord Jesus' flesh, there go your symptoms and condition. Lift up the cup and proclaim that His blood gives you life. Even if you have been a slave to endless rounds of treatment and medication for as long as you can remember, His finished work has made a way for you to receive your miracle.

TODAY'S PRAYER

Lord Jesus, thank You that You want me to rest while You fight my battles and overcome every enemy. Thank You for paying the price for my wholeness and giving me victory over even seemingly impossible conditions. I will take Your hand and let You lead me through my situation to the place where I never see the oppressive symptoms ever again. Amen.

DAY 59

HOLD ON TO GOD'S PROMISES

"Behold, all those who were incensed against you
Shall be ashamed and disgraced;
They shall be as nothing,
And those who strive with you shall perish.
You shall seek them and not find them—
Those who contended with you.
Those who war against you
Shall be as nothing,
As a nonexistent thing.
For I, the LORD your God, will hold your right hand,
Saying to you, 'Fear not, I will help you.'"

—Isaiah 41:11–13

Let me share with you a testimony I believe will greatly encourage you. One of my leaders was diagnosed with Meniere's disease when he suddenly suffered bouts of intense vertigo that completely incapacitated him for hours. Whenever a vertigo attack occurred, waves of nausea would overtake him, and he would find himself throwing up uncontrollably. He would also experience symptoms of tinnitus regularly, where every sound around him became magnified or distorted, and he could not hear what people were saying to him.

It was terrifying for him because the attacks were sudden and unpredictable, could happen while he was driving, and left him retching and vomiting until he was exhausted. It felt like he was trapped in the churning waters of a violent storm. His doctors told him that medication could help manage the symptoms, but there was no cure for his condition and the symptoms were, in fact, likely to get worse.

Then one day the Lord led him to the above passage from Isaiah 41. He said, "When God gave me that word, I kept meditating on it and kept it in my spirit. The words 'shall be as a nonexistent thing' kept jumping out at me, and I *knew* that I had it. I was healed."

He did not see the full manifestation of his healing immediately, but he had faith he was already healed *because of the word he received*. Faith is the substance of things hoped for, "the evidence of things not seen" (Heb. 11:1). So even before he saw the reality, he *knew* he was healed.

He continued to partake of the holy Communion regularly, but he no longer did so out of any sense of fear the symptoms would become increasingly debilitating. Instead, he partook knowing he was *already* healed, and after some time, he "stopped experiencing the symptoms altogether." As I write this, he has been completely symptom-free for well over a year. All glory to our lovely Savior!

Isaiah 41:11–13 is such a powerful passage to meditate on if you are faced with the enemies of sickness and disease today. Doesn't it remind you of what the Lord did for the children of Israel when He split open the Red Sea for them even though it appeared like all was lost? The Lord is no respecter of persons. Put your trust in Him. He can make a way when there seems to be no way. If He did it for the children of Israel, and He did it for the brother in my church, He can do it for you too.

TODAY'S THOUGHT

Even before this brother stopped experiencing symptoms in his body, he had faith he was already healed *because of the word he received*. He fought every battle of fear and unbelief armed with that verse from the Lord, and that is what I want to encourage you to do too. Find promises from the Lord for you in the Scriptures and hold on to them, for His Word is life to all who find them and health to all their flesh (Prov. 4:22).

TODAY'S PRAYER

Father, thank You for giving me Your precious, unshakable Word that is life and health to all my flesh. I ask You to open my eyes to Your many powerful promises that speak of what Jesus accomplished on the cross. I believe that as I receive and hold on to Your promises every symptom of disease in my body will be a nonexistent thing. Amen.

DAY 60

GOD'S WORD BRINGS LIFE AND HEALING

He sent His word and healed them,
And delivered them from their destructions.

—Psalm 107:20

I have received many healing testimonies where precious individuals were healed as they clung to specific promises in God's Word for them. Some years ago, I preached on 1 John 4:17, which says, "As He is, so are we in this world." Our Lord Jesus bore our sins and our diseases in His own body on the cross, and He rose from the grave without them. This means that as Jesus is without any disease, so are we in this world.

The following week a lady in my church received a medical report for a mammogram that showed a lump in her breast. Her doctors told her to come back in so they could conduct a biopsy. Her response was to write on the report, "As Jesus is, so am I in this world. Lord Jesus, do You have lumps in Your breast?" And then she prayed, "Lord, as You are free from lumps, so am I in this world." That's all. Just a simple prayer.

At her appointment, the doctors checked her and rechecked her, but could not find the lump or offer any explanation for how the lump could have simply disappeared! We don't need to know how; we just need to know who. It was our Jesus who healed her. Hallelujah!

I have received testimonies from so many people who were encouraged by this lady's praise report. They stood on this same scripture and kept confessing it over themselves until they received their breakthroughs. I really believe that reading testimonies is God's way. This is why the Bible is filled with so many healing testimonies for our benefit.

There is no healing too big or too small for the Lord. Testimonies from Peter's mother-in-law who was healed of fever (Matt. 8:14–15), to the man with the withered hand (Matt. 12:9–13), to the woman who could not stand up straight for eighteen years (Luke 13:11–13) were all recorded for us. There are praise reports of blind eyes healed (John 9:1–7; Mark 8:22–25; Luke 18:35–43; Matt. 9:27–30), deaf ears opened (Mark 7:32–35), and the mute speaking (Matt. 9:32–33). There are testimonies of those who had died being brought back to life (John 11:1–44; Mark 5:35–42).

Healing accounts are also recorded in the Old Testament. Naaman was healed of leprosy (2 Kings 5:1–14). Hezekiah was told he would not recover from a terminal illness, but God healed him and extended his life by fifteen years (2 Kings 20:1–7). And these are just a few of the many testimonies recorded for us in the Word of God.

Beloved, I want you to know that this can be your story and testimony too. What the Lord did for them, He can and will do for you! Jesus' healing for you rests on the foundation of His unchanging Word. Today let His healing and wholeness be manifested in your life as you anchor your heart in His promises, His perfect work, and His grace.

TODAY'S THOUGHT

Whatever you might be facing, my prayer for you is that the testimonies in this book will deposit faith in you. Our Lord Jesus told His disciples that if they had faith like a mustard seed, nothing would be impossible for them (Matt. 17:20). Do you know how small a mustard seed is? It is quite literally a tiny speck. And that's all you need!

TODAY'S PRAYER

Father God, thank You that You send forth Your Word and bring healing and deliverance. Thank You for every testimony from different individuals and for the abundance of praise reports in Your Word of healings of all kinds that show me Your will is for me to be completely healed and well. Let Your Word begin to make rich deposits of faith in me. I anchor my faith for my healing in Your promises and Your love for me. Amen.

DAY 61

BY THE WORD OF THEIR TESTIMONY

And they overcame him by the blood of the Lamb and by the word of their testimony, and they did not love their lives to the death.

—Revelation 12:11

Over the years, countless praise reports from people who were healed as they kept partaking of the holy Communion by faith have come into my ministry office. Someone gave a detailed account of how her father, who had been near death in an intensive care unit, improved each time they partook of the holy Communion on his behalf. It started with his kidney functions being partially restored, then his heart rate and blood pressure stabilized, and then he was able to breathe independently. Finally, he was discharged and celebrated his eighty-sixth birthday at his favorite restaurant. Even his doctor admitted his recovery was a miracle.

Several testimonies came in from people who were healed of cancer. A brother who developed inflammation of the brain and was given a very low chance of surviving was healed. Someone else testified of how she delivered a healthy baby without Down syndrome despite receiving reports that her baby would have this genetic disorder. Another person who had dealt with constant pain after breaking her hip was healed. A baby who was born ten weeks premature and struggled with multiple health problems was healed. There were those who were healed of severe anxiety attacks, deep depression, and sleep disorders. There were testimonies from people healed of lupus, asthma, skin conditions, tumors, gastric pains, and many other conditions.

My friend, Jesus is the same yesterday, today, and forever, and He continues to heal today. It doesn't matter what your medical challenge is. He can heal you. The holy Communion is not a gimmick; it is not a ritual; it is not a sentimental custom. It is the greatest expression of God's love. When you partake of the bread with this revelation, you release your faith to receive His health and wholeness in exchange for your sicknesses and diseases. When you drink the cup, you are reminded that the blood of the sinless Son of God didn't just bring you forgiveness, but it also made you eternally righteous, holy, and blameless. So today you have perfect standing before the Father, and His ears are attentive to your softest sigh.

Maybe you don't have faith to believe the medical condition in your body will disappear immediately. But can you have faith to believe He really loves you? That He really is as good as the Word says He is? Then let's start with that. I believe the more you read testimonies of His goodness and faithfulness and the more you immerse yourself in hearing all about Jesus and His finished work, the more faith for your healing will come.

TODAY'S THOUGHT

If you are believing God for a breakthrough, you can draw encouragement from many more praise reports found on our website at JosephPrince.com/eat. I am believing that as you partake of the Communion wholeheartedly receiving the Lord's love, you, too, will have an awesome testimony to share. And when you receive your breakthrough, please send me your praise report using the form at JosephPrince.com/eat. Your shared testimony will ignite the faith of others for their breakthroughs.

TODAY'S PRAYER

Lord Jesus, thank You that You are the same healer yesterday, today, and forever. I receive Your love for me as I partake of the holy Communion. I receive Your health and wholeness in exchange for my sicknesses. You have made me eternally righteous, and I come boldly to You to receive my healing. Amen.

SECTION IX

DON'T GIVE UP!

I would have lost heart, unless I had believed
That I would see the goodness of the Lord
In the land of the living.
—Psalm 27:13

DAY 62

HOW MUCH LONGER?

How long, O Lord? Will You forget me forever?
How long will You hide Your face from me?
How long shall I take counsel in my soul,
Having sorrow in my heart daily?
How long will my enemy be exalted over me?

—Psalm 13:1–2

I hope you have had the chance to read some of the testimonies on our website at JosephPrince.com/eat. Aren't you glad we have a God of miracles and that He continues to heal, save, and deliver today?

But maybe you have been partaking of the holy Communion for some time, yet nothing seems to be happening. Maybe you are tired of hearing about the testimonies of others because you can't help but think, *How about me, Lord? Have You forgotten about me? When am I going to receive my healing? How long do I have to wait?*

Beloved, I want you to know it is okay for you to cry out to the Lord and to ask, "How long, Lord?" That's what the psalmist David did in the verses above, and we get to read the words he poured out to the Lord in his anguish.

God loves you and He cares for you. He knows the discouragement that overwhelms you when it feels like the enemy of sickness has had the upper hand over you for so long and God feels so far away. He isn't shocked when you express such thoughts. He wants you to run to Him even when you have such thoughts. He knows exactly what you are going through and the despair that seems to be crushing you. Just bring it all to the Lord, but don't stay in that place of discouragement.

Continue reading what David wrote. Psalm 13 ends with this: "But I have trusted in Your mercy; my heart shall rejoice in Your salvation. I will sing to the LORD, because He has dealt bountifully with me" (Ps. 13:5–6).

But.

One little word that makes all the difference.

It may feel like hopelessness might overcome you, *but* don't give up. In the original Hebrew, the word the psalmist David used for *mercy* is *hesed* (grace), while the word used for *salvation* is *yeshua*. Keep trusting in His grace. Keep your eyes on your *Yeshua*, your Jesus. Your salvation—welfare, deliverance, and victory—is found in Him!

TODAY'S THOUGHT

As you talk to the Lord and spend time in His presence, you will find He does not give you the answer; He *is* the answer. At the cross, He purchased for us the gift of eternal life and healing, paid for with His own body and blood. Whatever saving or healing you need, Jesus *is* the answer.

TODAY'S PRAYER

Beloved Lord Jesus, thank You that You are my *Yeshua*, my sure salvation, my deliverer, and my healer. Thank You that You hear the cries of my heart and that Your grace has purchased my salvation and my healing. Even if my outward circumstances don't seem to change, I declare that You are the answer, and I will trust in You. Amen.

DAY 63
SELAH MOMENTS

Lord, how they have increased who trouble me!
Many are they who rise up against me.
Many are they who say of me,
"There is no help for him in God." Selah
But You, O Lord, are a shield for me,
My glory and the One who lifts up my head.

—Psalm 3:1–3

As you read what happened to David as he cried out to God in the verses above, notice the *selah* in the psalm. You will find such "*selah* moments" throughout David's psalms. That means David paused . . . and listened.

In those moments, David turned his eyes from his troubles and looked to his God. In those moments, I believe he remembered afresh that he did not have to fight his battles because the Lord of hosts fought for him (1 Sam. 17:45–47). He remembered afresh the God who had delivered him from the paw of the lion and the paw of the bear, the God who overcame Goliath without sword or spear. And as he looked to the Lord, he strengthened himself in the Lord (1 Sam. 30:6), and that's when things started to change.

Change came when he shifted his focus away from his painful and dire circumstances and allowed himself to be absorbed instead in the *grace* of the Lord, when he paused and tuned in to what the Lord was encouraging him with on the inside. I believe that in those few moments of meditating on God's goodness and mercy, he heard the Lord say to him, "David, why are you worried about all these people coming against you? *I* am your shield. *I* am the glory and the lifter of your head." That was what brought about David's turning point in the situation. God's comfort came to David as he chose to *selah*.

Does it seem like your enemies have increased and many are rising up against you? Have you been getting one bad report after another from the doctor? Maybe they have found a lot more to be concerned about than you were previously aware of. And now your heart is heavy because it feels like maybe even God can't help you.

At times like this, do what David did. *Selah*. Pause and choose to run to the Lord in the presence of your enemies.

When David came back to the psalm, his enemies were still there. But he could rise up and declare, "But You, O Lord, are a shield for me, my glory and the One who lifts up my head."

In your *selah* moments with the Lord, you will find your turning point and victory. Don't remain discouraged. Don't run away from Him. Run to Him and worship Him.

TODAY'S THOUGHT

If you don't know where to start in worshiping the Lord, may I invite you to join us? As a church we had a powerful, intimate, and liberating time worshiping with the psalms of David, and we would love for you to experience it too. You can do so by going to JosephPrince.com/eat. Exalt Him and His *hesed* (grace) instead of magnifying your challenges, and watch Him bring victory to your situation!

TODAY'S PRAYER

Glorious Lord Jesus, thank You for this *selah* moment when I can run to You and worship You. Thank You that You are a shield to me, my glory and the One who lifts my head high above my circumstances. There is nothing too hard for You. There is no enemy in my life that You have not already defeated. I exalt You and know that You will bring me through to victory. Amen.

DAY 64

LITTLE BY LITTLE

"I will not drive them out from before you in one year, lest the land become desolate and the beasts of the field become too numerous for you. Little by little I will drive them out from before you, until you have increased, and you inherit the land."

—Exodus 23:29–30

You can receive healing through the prayer of faith (Mark 11:24), and many times during our services, people are instantaneously healed as the gifts of healings flow (1 Cor. 12:9). There is a powerful corporate anointing at work when the church gathers together because Jesus said, "For where two or three are gathered together in My name, I am there in the midst of them" (Matt. 18:20). Where Jesus is, death turns into life and resurrection (John 11:25), weakness becomes strength, little becomes much, and in His presence is fullness of joy and pleasures forevermore (Ps. 16:11).

While I would love for everyone to receive immediate and complete healing all the time, you don't have to have an instantaneous manifestation or feel something tangibly happening in your body to know God is healing you. The moment you partake of the holy Communion in faith, your healing has begun.

Most people who have sent in their healing testimonies to my ministry weren't healed in a spectacular prayer meeting or when a man or woman of God laid hands on them. They were healed gradually by the

Lord as they partook of His ordained channel through which we receive His supernatural life and health—the holy Communion.

Sometimes teachings on the prayer of faith can put pressure on you to believe you have complete healing the moment you pray. But truth be told, most of us don't have that kind of faith. As for the gifts of healings, they operate as the Spirit wills (1 Cor. 12:11) and not as man wills. When it comes to the holy Communion, there is no pressure. Each time you partake in faith, you receive a measure of healing and get better and better.

Sometimes we get impatient and want the Lord to drive out all our enemies at once. Read the verses above from Exodus 23 and see what the Lord said to the children of Israel as they were preparing to enter the promised land. *Little by little. Little by little.*

Today we don't face the Hivites, Hittites, or Canaanites like the children of Israel did. But our enemies might be renal failure, leukemia, or high blood pressure. Whatever it is, don't be discouraged. The symptoms might still be there even though you have partaken of the holy Communion, but keep partaking. The manifestation of your healing is coming. The enemy is being driven out from your life. Your healing might not be taking place as quickly as you would like it to, but it is taking place. My friend, don't give up!

TODAY'S THOUGHT

Be patient and give yourself time to grow in God's grace and receive the healing He provides in the holy Communion, measure by measure. Just let your faith be anchored in His grace and let Him do His deep, lasting work in you. Your healing may not happen right away, but in time His grace that is at work in Your life will be evident to everyone. So never lose hope.

TODAY'S PRAYER

Lord Jesus, thank You that each time I come to You, I receive more and more of Your resurrection life. I believe that as I partake of the Communion, I am receiving more and more of Your healing power. Even if I can't see it or feel it, I believe You are doing a deep healing work in my body and that my complete healing will be manifested in Your time. Amen.

DAY 65
SUPERNATURAL BUT UNSPECTACULAR

So continuing daily with one accord in the temple, and breaking bread from house to house, they ate their food with gladness and simplicity of heart.

—Acts 2:46

There are times when someone partakes of the Lord's Supper and the healing that follows is immediate. But this is usually the exception rather than the rule. In most instances, the healing takes place gradually. Gradual does not mean healing is not happening.

Some years ago, I suffered a sharp pain in my tailbone each time I got up after sitting down, even if the chair was soft and cushioned. When I consulted a doctor, he told me it was wear and tear "due to age" and there was nothing I could do about it. When he said that, I realized my body was succumbing to the natural forces of aging.

But I refused to accept it because I am in this world but not of this world (John 17:11, 14). I *should not* be subject to what the world suffers. And neither should you. As we saw in section 8, Christ has redeemed us from the curse of the law and that includes all the diseases the world suffers. So I decided to avail myself of the Lord's provision and started partaking of the holy Communion for my tailbone pain.

Do you know what happened immediately after I partook of the holy Communion? I got up from my seat and intense pain shot through my body. The next day, I partook of the Lord's Supper again with the same results. This went on for some time. I would partake of the holy Communion, but the pain remained. Then one day, I suddenly realized I had stood up without flinching. In fact, when I thought about it, I realized I hadn't suffered any pain for a few days. I was healed!

The Lord had healed me supernaturally, but the healing took place so gradually, as I kept partaking of the Lord's Supper, that I did not immediately realize when I was healed or how long it had taken. I believe that is how most healings take place.

This is why our Lord Jesus said, "This do, as often as you drink it, in remembrance of Me" (1 Cor. 11:25). Notice He said "as often" and not "as rarely" or "as infrequently." That tells us He was referring to constantly partaking of the holy Communion. But how do we define "often"? The Lord leaves it to us to decide.

I just know this: the early church partook of the Communion *daily*, breaking bread from house to house. They must have had a revelation of how beneficial the Communion was to their bodies and partook of the Communion as often as they could. I am not saying we have to partake of it every day. But if you feel led to, then please do so by all means.

TODAY'S THOUGHT

Do not let a delay in your healing discourage you from partaking of the Lord's Supper often. Each time you partake of the holy Communion, you are looking to Jesus and receiving what He has accomplished on the cross to give you health, wholeness, and abundant life. Keep partaking and in time you will enjoy the full benefits of Jesus' broken body and shed blood.

TODAY'S PRAYER

Lord Jesus, thank You that You have redeemed me from the curse of sicknesses and diseases, which includes the conditions in my body right now. Even when I see no immediate results from partaking of the holy Communion, I thank You that does not mean my healing is not happening. I believe that gradual and unspectacular are still supernatural and my complete healing will manifest as I keep partaking often. Amen.

DAY 66

DO NOT CONSIDER YOUR OWN BODY

And not being weak in faith, [Abraham] did not consider his own body, already dead (since he was about a hundred years old), and the deadness of Sarah's womb.

—Romans 4:19

What should you do when you continue to be confronted with the symptoms or even when the enemy keeps reminding you of so-and-so who wasn't healed? Keep on partaking of the holy Communion and thanking the Lord that everything you need for your healing has already been supplied through the cross. Scripture tells us Christ has *already* redeemed you from the curse of every sickness and disease (Gal. 3:13).

When our Lord Jesus instituted the holy Communion, He took the cup and "gave thanks" (Matt. 26:27). The Greek word for *gave thanks* is *eucharisteo*, which means "to express gratitude."[1] This is why the holy Communion is also known as the Eucharist. You give thanks for something that is already done, that you have already received. So even if the symptoms are still in your body, you can give thanks and call yourself healed because His Word declares that "by His stripes we are healed" (Isa. 53:5).

Don't try to "get" healing for yourself or your loved one. It is already yours! The enemy has been conquered (Col. 2:15). Jesus has *already* given you divine health. Always remember this: as a believer, you do not fight for victory; you fight *from* victory.

My friend, let's be like Abraham, who was convinced God was able to do what He had promised. Even though Abraham was very advanced in years, he believed God's promise that He would make him a father of many nations and *did not consider his own body* or the deadness of his wife Sarah's womb. And you know the story: Isaac was born to Abraham when he was already one hundred years old (Gen. 21:5) and when Sarah was about ninety. In the natural, that was impossible as they were both past the natural childbearing age.

But Abraham did not consider the deadness of his own body; he considered God's promise. Romans 4:20–21 tells us he "did not waver at the promise of God through unbelief, but was strengthened in faith, giving glory to God, and being fully convinced that what He had promised He was also able to perform."

In the same way, may I encourage you to be like Abraham? *Do not consider* the symptoms of sickness in your body. Instead, fix your eyes on our Lord Jesus and consider the promise in God's Word, which declares that by Jesus' stripes you are *already* healed. Keep partaking of the Communion in faith, thanking Him that His body was broken so yours might be whole. And as you partake, like the children of Israel, get ready for and keep expecting your physical deliverance.

TODAY'S THOUGHT

We have God's promise that the full payment for our sins and sicknesses has already been made by our Lord Jesus' sacrifice at Calvary. Let the wonderful assurance that healing is already yours fill your heart, mind, and mouth!

TODAY'S PRAYER

Father, thank You that the enemy is defeated, and I fight from victory. I will not consider the symptoms in my body, but I will fix my eyes on Jesus and rest in the assurance that healing is mine. Thank You that each time I partake of the holy Communion, I am receiving a greater and greater measure of healing. In Jesus' name, amen.

DAY 67

WHEN YOU HAVE NO FAITH

By faith Sarah herself also received strength to conceive seed, and she bore a child when she was past the age, because she judged Him faithful who had promised.

—Hebrews 11:11

Perhaps you are at a place where you feel like you can't conjure up any more faith, let alone "not waver at the promise of God" like Abraham (Rom. 4:20). Maybe you are thinking, *I have tried and tried to believe for so long. I have no more faith to carry on.*

Let me show you what today's verse says about Sarah. There was faith involved when Sarah conceived and bore a child. But if you think faith is awfully hard and that you simply have no faith, I pray this will encourage you.

How did Sarah receive her miracle after so long and when it seemed impossible in the natural? She "judged Him faithful who had promised." It seems so simple, but therein lay her miracle. The faith walk isn't hard. It is easy and effortless. When your faith runs out, judge God faithful. When you do not know how to have faith anymore, reckon on *His* faithfulness. Remember that *He* is faithful. Lean on *His* faithfulness.

Don't give up because you think you don't have enough faith. Once God gives you a promise, it is not for you to conjure up faith. It is for you to rest in the One who promised, knowing that He is faithful.

There is a beautiful verse I want you to emblazon across your spirit that will steady you in the fight of faith when it seems like your answers are not forthcoming: "If we are faithless, He remains faithful; He cannot deny Himself" (2 Tim. 2:13). Even when you are faithless, He remains faithful. At the cross, as Jesus carried all our sins, God the Father had to turn away from His Son, and Jesus cried out, "My God, My God, why have You forsaken Me?" (Matt. 27:46). He paid the price for you and me to have God's constant presence, and because of that, God will never leave you nor forsake you (Heb. 13:5). He will never relax His hold on you. When you feel faithless, know that you don't have to try to hold on to Him—He is the One holding on to you. The Bible says the Lord your God holds your right hand, saying to you, "Fear not, I will help you" (Isa. 41:13).

When you have no more strength to even have faith in your battle with your sickness, may I encourage you to do this? Take time to go into the Lord's presence and tell Him:

Lord Jesus, thank You for Your faithfulness to me. You are faithful in Your goodness to carry out Your promises in my life. You are faithful to heal me and to restore to me every bit of health and well-being I have lost through this sickness. Right now, because You are faithfully upholding me, I can let go and rest in You. It is Your faithfulness that will cause my healing to manifest. Amen.

TODAY'S THOUGHT

Beloved, just talking to Jesus like that *is* faith to Him. It is believing He is in your situation with you and that He is listening. And as you declare over the symptoms in your body that the One who has promised you healing is faithful, you are judging Him faithful, and you will see Him faithfully causing your healing to manifest.

TODAY'S PRAYER

Beloved Lord Jesus, thank You for Your promise that even when I feel I have no faith to carry on, You remain faithful. Thank You that because You paid the price for me, healing for every condition in my body is my right and my portion. I will rest in You, knowing that You will be faithful to cause my healing to manifest. Amen.

DAY 68

DON'T CONFUSE FAITH WITH EMOTIONS

For we walk by faith, not by sight.

—2 Corinthians 5:7

Some years ago, the wife of one of my key leaders was diagnosed with a cyst in her womb that the doctors said had to be removed by surgery. She was told they might even have to remove her whole womb. Of course, this couple was very affected by the news. I met with them to pray with them and to partake of the holy Communion.

Honestly, I didn't feel any faith when I prayed for them. In fact, I felt quite helpless. But I heard the Lord telling me to rest. I heard Him telling me not to even try to use faith and to simply rest in His faith. So I simply said, "Growth, I curse you to your roots in Jesus' name. Be plucked out by your roots and be thrown into the sea." At the same time, I also prayed the Lord would cause her youth to be renewed like the eagle's.

A few days later, she had a final scan before her surgery. And guess what? Her gynecologist said the whole growth had simply disappeared and that it was a miracle! But the Lord didn't stop there. Her monthly period had actually stopped for some time, but soon after I prayed for her, it returned. The Lord had renewed her womb and her youth. Hallelujah!

I felt no faith when I prayed for her, but her healing was not dependent on what I felt about my faith. Don't look at your own faith and think, *I don't have enough faith for the breakthrough I need*. Faith is nothing more than looking to Jesus. There were only two individuals in the Gospels whom Jesus described as having "great faith": the centurion who believed Jesus only had to speak a word and his servant at home would be healed (Matt. 8:5–13) and the Syro-Phoenician woman to whom Jesus said, "O woman, great is your faith!" (Matt. 15:21–28).

And neither of them was conscious of their own faith.

Do you want to know what they were conscious of? They were conscious of Jesus. They saw Him as the One who was faithful and powerful. They had a great estimation of His grace and goodness. And as they saw Him in His grace, He saw them in their faith!

Don't worry about whether or not you have enough faith. Just look to Jesus. Spend time in His presence. Watch or listen to sermons that are full of Jesus. When you touch Jesus, you touch faith because He is the author and finisher of faith (Heb. 12:2). The Bible declares He is faithful, and He will not allow you to go through more than what you can bear (1 Cor. 10:13). He will carry you through.

TODAY'S THOUGHT

Healing is not dependent on your faith; it is dependent on the faith of the faithful One, our Lord Jesus. That's why the holy Communion is so powerful. It puts your focus on Jesus and on Him alone. Even if you don't feel any faith when you are partaking of the holy Communion, don't stop. Don't focus on your faith or lack of it. Sometimes we confuse faith with emotions. Just put your trust in the One who never wavers. Don't give up!

TODAY'S PRAYER

Father in heaven, thank You that healing is not dependent on whether I feel I have enough faith or even any faith. Thank You that my faith is only dependent on looking to Jesus and focusing on Him and what He has accomplished for me. As I partake of the holy Communion, help me to see more and more of His grace and to rest in His faithfulness to carry me through. Amen.

TESTIMONY

Healed of Incurable Neuromuscular Disease

Several years ago, I was diagnosed with myasthenia gravis (a chronic autoimmune disorder characterized by muscular weakness). It started with weak eyelids, and I couldn't open my eyes fully. This made me look as if I was drunk or doped up on drugs. I was told that in the advanced stages, I could lose my ability to walk and eventually not be able to swallow.

An eye specialist and two neurosurgeons confirmed the diagnosis. There is no known cure for the condition and the doctors told me they could only help delay its progression and manage the symptoms with lifelong medication. I cried and found it hard to trust God for healing.

MY HUSBAND WOULD SIT ME DOWN EVERY NIGHT, AND WE WOULD PARTAKE OF THE HOLY COMMUNION TOGETHER. IN SPITE OF MY FEARS, I FOUND GREAT COMFORT EACH TIME WE PARTOOK OF THE HOLY COMMUNION.

However, my husband and I continued to listen to Pastor Prince's sermons in church and while commuting to work every day.

My husband would sit me down every night to pray for healing, and we would partake of the holy Communion together. In spite of my fears, I found great comfort each time we partook of the holy Communion. Some days I had no words to pray, and he would encourage me to repeat after him, giving thanks to God for the priceless and powerful sacrifice of

Jesus at Calvary. We claimed God's promises in Psalm 23 that we would have no lack and that we would lead healthy and fruitful lives.

Two days before my appointment with the neurosurgeon, I was taken off all my medication. To our surprise, the neurosurgeon noticed that my eyelids were not drooping. He next asked me to stand so he could check my muscle strength. Then looking perplexed, he asked if I had stopped taking the medication. When I said yes, he commented that without medication for more than twenty-four hours, it was impossible that my eyelids were not drooping. So he cancelled the further tests that were to be conducted and confirmed that there were no symptoms of myasthenia gravis.

I was overjoyed and declared that I was healed by Christ Jesus! That was the last time I needed to see a doctor for myasthenia gravis. All glory be to God! My husband and I are so grateful for Pastor Prince's ministry that has opened our eyes and ears to the wonderful gospel of grace.

Corrine | Singapore

SECTION X

THE FIGHT TO REST

Finally, my brethren, be strong in the Lord and in the power of His might. Put on the whole armor of God, that you may be able to stand against the wiles of the devil. For we do not wrestle against flesh and blood, but against principalities, against powers, against the rulers of the darkness of this age, against spiritual hosts of wickedness in the heavenly places. Therefore take up the whole armor of God, that you may be able to withstand in the evil day, and having done all, to stand.

—Ephesians 6:10–13

DAY 69

SPIRITUAL WARFARE

For we do not wrestle against flesh and blood, but against principalities, against powers, against the rulers of the darkness of this age, against spiritual hosts of wickedness in the heavenly places.

—Ephesians 6:12

I don't know if you realize it, but we are engaged in warfare. In our modern world, many of us have access to doctors, hospitals, and various medications and treatments. And because we can just turn to Google for information about our symptoms and find out all about possible causes and treatment options, it is easy for us to forget there is an invisible realm. It is easy to forget there is a real enemy and that spiritual forces could be involved when we find ourselves under attack in our bodies.

There is an enemy who wants to destroy us, to oppress us with sickness, and to stop us from reaping the harvest of health and divine life that is our inheritance as believers. I am not saying all diseases are caused by spirits, but let's not forget spirits exist. The gospel of Luke records how our Lord Jesus healed a woman who had been oppressed by a "spirit of infirmity" (Luke 13:10–17). For eighteen years she was bent over and could not raise herself up. Our Lord Jesus Himself said it was because *Satan* had bound her.

Thank God for doctors and nurses who have dedicated their lives to caring for the sick, preventing diseases, and alleviating the sufferings of their patients. They are a great blessing, and I fully believe God can work through them. But there is a limit to what doctors can do when spiritual forces are involved, and we cannot use *natural* means to come against *supernatural* forces.

The apostle Paul wrote that our fight is not "against flesh and blood," our warfare is a spiritual one. For most people, spiritual warfare conjures up the idea of engaging in fierce battles with the devil. But some years ago, when I wrote a book titled *Spiritual Warfare*, do you know what I chose as the image for the cover of the book? A picture of a man lying on a deck chair by the beach, with his arms folded languidly behind his head.

It's important to note that the whole passage about spiritual warfare in Ephesians 6 tells us over and over again to "stand" and mentions fighting only once, when it tells us that we do not "wrestle against flesh and blood" (Eph. 6:11–14). Our fight is the fight to remain at rest and believe the work has already been finished. The only labor is the labor to enter the rest our Lord Jesus purchased for us at the cross (Heb. 4:11 KJV).

TODAY'S THOUGHT

While I am not going to delve into teaching about spiritual warfare in the following readings, I will show you by example what it means to engage in spiritual warfare. God's Word tells us that our part in the warfare is to *stand still* and see the salvation of the Lord (Ex. 14:13; 2 Chron. 20:17). Let's stand in the victory Christ has already given us, instead of trying to defeat a foe that has *already* been defeated at the cross.

TODAY'S PRAYER

Father, thank You that no matter what thoughts, imaginations, or symptoms oppress me, I can stand upon the great truth that victory is firmly secured through Jesus' finished work. Thank You that my only fight is to remain at rest, knowing that the enemy has already been defeated at the cross. Thank You that because I am Your child, all I need to do is to stand still and see Your salvation. Amen.

DAY 70

WHAT SPIRITUAL WARFARE LOOKS LIKE

"You come to me with a sword, with a spear, and with a javelin. But I come to you in the name of the LORD of hosts, the God of the armies of Israel, whom you have defied."

—1 Samuel 17:45

To show you what it means to engage in spiritual warfare, let me share with you the precious journey taken by Anna, who was part of our ministry team for my Grace Revolution Tour. While she was in Dallas, Texas, she went through a horrifying ordeal.

She recounted experiencing a numbness in her legs that quickly progressed to her diaphragm. Unable to move, she was rushed to the emergency room where she underwent a five-hour emergency surgery for spinal cord compression caused by multiple lesions and tumorous growths along her entire spinal cord. Without warning, she found herself bedridden with stage-four cancer that had metastasized from the thoracic area to her neck and bones. Given a life expectancy of three years, this is how she described her battle:

All that I, a frightened sheep, could do was to just stay really close to the Great Shepherd. During my entire thirty-three days of hospitalization, Jesus became my impenetrable "safe house," protecting me from further assaults by the devil. I requested for visitors to be kept

> *to a minimum, choosing to spend the time with the One whose very presence and words were now my very life and healing. Just hearing the way the doctors and nurses talked about my cancer caused the life and peace in me to leak—I felt that I had touched death.*
>
> *But I remained in my "safe house," Jesus. I fed on God's Word during my waking hours, often drifting off to sleep with Pastor Prince's sermons playing on my iPad. Every time I took my cancer medication, and after undergoing each round of radiotherapy, I would also partake of the holy Communion. I believe that was the reason I didn't experience* any *of the side effects, except for temporary hair loss, throughout my fifteen cycles of radiotherapy treatment. I just continued daily in the Word and in partaking of the holy Communion.*

The cancer was real, but Anna knew the true battle was a spiritual one. Of course, she was fearful. But she is a child of God and was not going to take the enemy's attacks lying down or allow him to intimidate her. She fought back, armed with the sword of the Spirit (Eph. 6:17), knowing that her God was backing her up all the way.

Anna reminds me of how David refused to cow in fear before the giant Goliath as the other soldiers of Israel did. Rather, he got *angry* and demanded to know "who is this uncircumcised Philistine, that he should defy the armies of the living God?" (1 Sam. 17:26). David was conscious only of how big his God was. The enemy may come against you with a sword, spear, and javelin, but when you come to him in the name of the Lord of hosts, that Goliath is no match for your God!

TODAY'S THOUGHT

Beloved, if the enemy is trying to attack you with symptoms, I pray you catch David's spirit. Don't be afraid. Stand your ground and know that the enemy has already been defeated. His weapons might appear formidable to the world, but greater is He who is in you than he who is in the world (1 John 4:4 KJV). This battle is not yours to fight.

TODAY'S PRAYER

Lord Jesus, thank You that You are also my "safe house," the Lord of hosts, in whose presence is my very life and healing. Thank You that no matter what weapon the enemy brings against me, the enemy is no match for You. I stand my ground and rest in the victory You have already given me. Amen.

DAY 71

FORTIFIED WITH THE WORD OF GOD

Sanctify them by Your truth. Your word is truth.

—John 17:17

Coming back to Anna's journey, at times some of the dire medical facts caused the life and peace in her to "leak." But instead of accepting these facts, she put on the full armor of God by standing resolutely on His finished work. Beyond that, she kept herself in the secret place of the Most High, allowing Him to be her refuge and fortress, taking Him as her deliverer (Ps. 91:1–3), and making Him her "impenetrable safe house" and her ark. He was her strong tower, her shield, and her Great Shepherd who protected her and carried her close to His heart.

She did not want to hear the groans of the other patients and the constant beeping of all the medical instruments in her ward or to keep looking at the death and sickness around her. So she girded herself with the truth of the Word of God, meditating on scriptures throughout the day, listening to sermons, and partaking of the holy Communion daily.

She stood on the eternal *truth* of the living Word, declaring scriptures that spoke to specific attack points of the cancer, such as, "It shall come to pass in that day that *his burden will be taken away from your shoulder, and his yoke from your neck*, and the yoke will be destroyed because of the anointing oil" (Isa. 10:27). And she stood firmly on other healing scriptures, such as, "And if Christ is in you, the body is dead because of sin, but *the Spirit is life* because of righteousness. But if the Spirit of Him who raised Jesus from the dead dwells in you, *He who raised Christ from the dead will also give life to your mortal bodies* through His Spirit who dwells in you" (Rom. 8:10–11).

As Anna kept feeding herself with scripture after scripture, I believe the Word of God literally became like medicine to her, and she grew stronger and stronger. When you spend time in the Word of God, you can't help but reap its healing benefits. After all, the book of Proverbs tells us that His words are "life to those who find them, and health to all their flesh" (Prov. 4:22). The Hebrew word for *health* is *marpe'*, which also means "a medicine" or "a cure."[1] Notice that the Word of God is "health to *all* their flesh." Unlike many medications, the Word of God does not benefit one part of your body only to harm another part. It is health to your nose, to your knees, to your inner ear, to your intestines, to your skin—to *all* your flesh.

TODAY'S THOUGHT

Whatever condition you are faced with, I encourage you to do what Anna did. Saturate yourself with the Word any way you can. Write out scriptures, listen to your audio Bible, listen to sermons about His finished work, and read books (like this one) that magnify all Jesus has done for you. Then take your stand upon His words of promise and wait patiently until it takes root and brings you your harvest of healing.

TODAY'S PRAYER

Most High God, thank You that I can hide myself in You, for You are my refuge and fortress, my strong tower, my shield, and my deliverer. Thank You that I have Your Word of truth and Your exceedingly great promises of healing to stand upon. I believe Your Word is health and life to me, and I will saturate myself in the Word as I wait patiently for my harvest of health. Amen.

DAY 72

THE POWER OF GOD'S WORD

For the word of God is living and powerful, and sharper than any two-edged sword, piercing even to the division of soul and spirit, and of joints and marrow.

—Hebrews 4:12

The Bible declares that the Word of God is the opposite of death—it is *living* and *powerful*. No wonder our Lord Jesus, when explaining the parable of the sower, tells us that when the sower sows the Word, "Satan comes immediately and takes away the word that was sown in their hearts" (Mark 4:15).

Did you notice that the enemy comes *immediately*? Jesus was referring to the seeds that "fell by the wayside," but the principle I want you to see is that the enemy wants to steal the Word from our hearts because he does not want you to "believe and be saved" (Luke 8:5, 12). The devil knows that if you receive the Word and believe it, *you will be saved*. This is why he will do all he can to stop the Word of God from taking root in your heart. He knows that if it stays long enough, it will be your victory and his defeat!

The word used for *saved* in the original Greek is the word *sozo*, which means "to save one from injury or peril; to save a suffering one from perishing, for example, one suffering from disease; to make well, heal, restore to health."[1]

The enemy knows how potent the Word of God is. Do you? No matter what channel you use to spend time in His Word, make sure you are well watered with the Word. As you keep yourself drenched and watered with the Word of God, I believe you will unconsciously and effortlessly get stronger and stronger, healthier and healthier.

Anna's healing did not come overnight, and your healing might also not be immediate, but believe that it is on its way. If you have been waiting for a while for your healing and you are feeling discouraged, let this promise from God strengthen you:

> *"For as the rain comes down, and the snow from heaven, and do not return there, but water the earth, and make it bring forth and bud, that it may give seed to the sower and bread to the eater, so shall My word be that goes forth from My mouth; it shall not return to Me void, but it shall accomplish what I please, and it shall prosper in the thing for which I sent it." (Isa. 55:10–11)*

God's Word of healing is so powerful that it will not return to Him void, but it shall accomplish His purpose. Maybe you have partaken of the Communion, and you have prayed, but nothing seems to be happening. You may even feel like you are just going through the motions because discouragement has set in. What do you do? Keep on watering the seed of the Word of God with the rain of His Word. Don't give up. The harvest is coming!

TODAY'S THOUGHT

Abraham saw God's promise of him having a son come to pass only after he had "patiently endured" (Heb. 6:13–15). There was a fight of faith involved. The blessing did not manifest the next day or even in the next year, but it was watered for many years.

The principle is that it might take some time, but you *will* inherit your promise as you hold on to God's Word.

TODAY'S PRAYER

Father, thank You that Your Word is living and powerful to save me from any disease and restore me to fullness of health. Thank You that Your Word will not return to You void, but it will prosper in Your purpose to heal. I will water myself with the rain of Your Word and keep partaking of the Communion for the harvest that I know is coming. Amen.

DAY 73

FAITH AND MEDICINE

You will keep him in perfect peace,
Whose mind is stayed on You,
Because he trusts in You.

—Isaiah 26:3

Anna's healing took place slowly but surely. She was bedridden for nine whole months and had to slowly learn to walk again. After going through radiotherapy treatment, she also had to go through hormonal chemotherapy. But she kept holding on to the Lord's promises and partaking of the Communion, remembering all He had done for her. Today she walks around freely without any aids. It took two years, but she is now back at work in my ministry office. And every opportunity she gets to pray for her colleagues who are unwell, she grabs. Indeed, the Lord has strengthened her and lengthened her days.

As for the cancer, her tumor marker has fallen way below the acceptable reading of <35.0 U/ml. The Lord used medical technology in her healing process, but as she continues "daily in the Word and in partaking of the holy Communion," He has kept her protected from the negative side effects of the radiation and medication that many others have experienced. Hallelujah! All glory to Jesus!

It is vital for believers to understand that faith in the Lord's healing power doesn't mean you don't seek medical advice or that you discontinue your medical treatment. Faith and medicine don't have to be mutually exclusive. In fact, I believe God uses doctors, and I have nothing but respect and honor for them. I have taught my church to pray that the Lord will anoint the hands of their surgeons if they have to undergo surgery and that the Lord will give their doctors the wisdom to give accurate diagnoses and decide on the best treatments. Praise the Lord for all the advancements made in medical science. They have done so much to improve the quality of our lives and to help people live longer.

In Anna's case, her doctors were rightfully fulfilling their responsibilities by informing her of the possible side effects of the treatments they were about to put her through. But while she went ahead with the treatments, her confidence for her total healing and complete restoration was entirely in her Savior and the Shepherd of her soul, our Lord Jesus Christ. She put her trust wholly in the Lord and in the holy Communion, believing she would not experience negative side effects. And praise the Lord, she experienced minimal side effects. If you are struggling with this conflict of faith versus medicine, I pray Anna's living testimony will be a great source of encouragement to you and help you experience His supernatural peace.

TODAY'S THOUGHT

Faith isn't about throwing away your medication, stopping your prescribed treatments, or avoiding surgical procedures. Doctors and medical professionals are fighting the same battles against sickness and disease that we are. If your doctor has prescribed medicines or treatments for you, please continue to take them together with the holy Communion, knowing that your trust is ultimately in your Lord Jesus to protect and heal you.

TODAY'S PRAYER

Lord Jesus, thank You for how You use medical professionals to help keep and restore health, and I ask You to always give my doctors wisdom to make accurate diagnoses. But my confidence for total healing and restoration is in You alone. I trust wholly in You and as I partake of the holy Communion, I look to You to protect my body and bring about my healing. To You, Lord Jesus, be all the glory! Amen.

DAY 74

YOUR HUNDREDFOLD HARVEST IS COMING

"But these are the ones sown on good ground, those who hear the word, accept it, and bear fruit: some thirtyfold, some sixty, and some a hundred."

—Mark 4:20

When you get discouraged that you have been partaking of the holy Communion but your healing is taking longer than you hope for, the enemy can start to play mind games with you. Maybe you are starting to entertain thoughts that the Communion is just an empty ritual. May I tell you there is spiritual warfare going on to get you to give up on the very channel God has ordained to bring supernatural life and health into your body?

As I mentioned previously, miracles of instantaneous healing *can* take place. But our Lord Jesus tells us in today's scripture what to expect when we are trusting Him for a breakthrough that does not manifest instantly. Notice what He says about how the seeds of the Word of God bear fruit when they fall on good ground. Luke's gospel also records: "But as for that seed in the good soil, these are the ones who have heard the word with a good and noble heart, and *hold on to it tightly, and bear fruit with patience*" (Luke 8:15 AMP).

The seeds that fall on good ground "bear fruit with patience." "Patience" refers to perseverance and endurance. Do you know why patience is involved? Because *it takes time for seeds to bear fruit.* It does not happen overnight. Just as the farmer waits patiently for the precious fruit of the earth, you also need to be patient (James 5:7). Your harvest will come incrementally—first thirtyfold, then sixtyfold, then a hundredfold.

When you begin to partake of the Communion, you might see some improvements, but the pain is mostly still there. That's a thirtyfold harvest. Don't give up! Keep on partaking of the holy Communion by faith until you get your sixtyfold harvest. That's when you know there has been major improvement—you can even feel it—but maybe some symptoms are still there, lingering on. That's the time to keep persevering, and to keep trusting, and to keep putting your eyes on His finished work until you see your hundredfold harvest of blessings, and you experience full healing for your condition.

When a seed is sown, you don't see anything immediately, but you know it will begin to sprout leaves and grow. You don't have to keep digging up the soil to check if the seed is growing. In the same way, when the seed of the Word of God is sown, your part is to have faith in the power of His Word and to be patient, as you believe that His words shall not return to Him void. And just as the earth yields crops incrementally, "first the blade, then the head, after that the full grain in the head" (Mark 4:28), I declare that you shall reap the full harvest of your healing!

TODAY'S THOUGHT

Please don't allow the enemy to sell you the lie that you should just give up partaking of the Communion because your healing is never going to happen. Keep on watering the seed of the Word of God and wait patiently until it takes root. In due season, you will surely reap your harvest (Gal. 6:9).

TODAY'S PRAYER

Heavenly Father, thank You that You are the One who sows the seeds of Your Word on the good ground of my heart. Thank You that I can keep putting my eyes on Jesus' finished work and partaking of the Communion until I receive my hundredfold harvest of a full healing. I believe in the power of Your Word, and I can hold on to it with patience, Father, because I know You are a faithful God. Amen.

DAY 75

THE GROUND IS READY FOR YOUR HEALING

"The plowers plowed on my back;
They made their furrows long."

—Psalm 129:3

While our Lord Jesus uses the analogy of the sower and the seed to teach us about the Word of God, in the verse above we also find a powerful and graphic agricultural imagery being used to help us understand the violent suffering He endured for our healing.

Psalm 129 is a messianic psalm, and this is a picture of the scourging our Lord Jesus went through. I was reading this verse one day, and I felt the Lord saying to me, "Meditate on why I used words that are associated with farming." That made me wonder, *Why did the Lord say, "They plowed My back" rather than beat, scourged, or hit?*

Plowers drag a sharp plow that digs into the soil to break up the soil and make deep furrows in preparation for seeds to be sown as pictured on the following page. I believe that was what happened to our Lord Jesus' back. When He was scourged by the Roman soldiers, it was as if His whole back had been plowed.

Furrows made in the ground by a plow allow for the planting of seeds and irrigation. In Psalm 129, the furrows speak of the scourging Jesus received for our healing.

Victims of Roman flagellation were scourged using a whip made up of several long leather thongs embedded with shards of broken bone, metal, and hooks. With each stroke, the thongs would wrap around the victim's body, and the shards would lodge in his flesh. When it was jerked away, the flesh of the victim would be ripped off and left in shreds, making deep, long furrows across his back.[1] By the time our Lord's tormentors were done, I believe there wasn't a single sliver of skin left on His back. Psalm 22, a messianic psalm, tells us that even His bones were exposed and stared back at Him (Ps. 22:17).

It was not by coincidence the language of sowing was used to describe our Lord Jesus' horrific scourging. Furrows are made so seeds can be sown. When you feel like you have no faith to believe in healing, our Lord Jesus says you just need faith as small as a mustard seed (Luke 17:6). It is not about how strong your faith is—just sow your little seeds of faith into the good ground of our Lord. The more you see what He has done for you, the more your faith will grow and the more you will experience a harvest of healing.

When His back was lashed into furrows, He was allowing the seed for your specific healing to be sown, whether it is high blood pressure, a tumor, or your child's asthma. Whatever condition you or your loved one might be suffering from, Jesus' suffering and sacrifice speak of how the price for your healing has been paid in full. It speaks of how you are so loved. Now reach out by faith and receive your healing. And even as you wait for your hundredfold harvest, may you experience His love for you like never before!

TODAY'S THOUGHT

Whenever you partake of the Communion, remember our Lord Jesus suffered every sickness, every physical pain, and every mental sorrow on your behalf in His own body. He was wounded for your sins and transgressions. He was crushed for your iniquities. The punishment with a view to your health and well-being fell upon Him. And by His stripes *you are healed* (Isa. 53:4–5).

TODAY'S PRAYER

Beloved Lord Jesus, thank You for bearing the terrible scourging as Your back was lashed into furrows for my sake. I receive Your love for me afresh as I see Your sacrifice for me. I thank You that by faith I can put my specific need for healing into Your good ground and know that the price has been paid in full. As I continue to partake of the Communion, I declare that by Your stripes I am healed. Amen.

SECTION XI

GOD OF YOUR VALLEYS

Then a man of God came and spoke to the king of Israel, and said, "Thus says the Lord: 'Because the Syrians have said, "The Lord is God of the hills, but He is not God of the valleys," therefore I will deliver all this great multitude into your hand, and you shall know that I am the Lord.'"

—1 Kings 20:28

DAY 76

HE IS WITH YOU

"I will never leave you nor forsake you."

—Hebrews 13:5

I pray your eyes have been opened to the amazing truths about the holy Communion and that you are excited about the revelations you have received. If you are facing a medical challenge, I pray the Lord has used this book to impart hope, life, and strength to you. Maybe you have even gathered the Communion elements and have started to partake of them. If so, praise the Lord! Keep persevering till you receive your breakthrough.

But maybe you are thinking, *I have read so many testimonies, and it feels like everyone else has received their breakthroughs and are experiencing their mountaintops. But where is God in my situation? Am I going to stay in this valley forever?*

Beloved, I want you to know He never leaves you nor forsakes you. He is near to those who are brokenhearted (Ps. 34:18), and right now He is drawn to you in your situation as you cry out to Him. He is both the God of the mountaintops and the God of the valleys (1 Kings 20:28). He is with you even in the valley, and because of that, you can have the confidence that you *will* get through it (Ps. 23:4).

I really believe knowing the truths about the holy Communion can mean the difference between life and death for you and your loved ones. In fact, I experienced the healing power of the holy Communion as I was writing *Eat Your Way to Life and Health.*

When my six-year-old son, Justin, fell from a structure in the schoolyard and hurt his head, my wife, Wendy, took him to the hospital for a thorough checkup. The doctors put him through a CT scan and discovered he had fractured his skull. After he started throwing up, a more detailed scan found a second fracture in his skull. They also discovered some bleeding in his skull as well as blood in his middle ear.

It was heart-wrenching for me to watch my little boy crying and clutching his head, twisting and turning in a vain attempt to stop the intense pain. It was also not easy for me to look at the scans and listen to his doctor talk about the possible effect of the injury on Justin's brain. Fear crept into my heart, and it was truly a fight to remain at rest.

Apart from giving him painkillers and monitoring him, the doctors couldn't do much for Justin. But Wendy and I knew God could, and during the entire period of his hospitalization, we partook of the Communion with him at least three or four times each day. Amazingly, every time we partook of the Communion with Justin, his headaches got less painful, and he got better and better. The doctors expected Justin to take at least six weeks to get better, but the Lord so accelerated his recovery that in less than three weeks, they gave him the all clear to return to school. All glory to Jesus!

TODAY'S THOUGHT

During what Justin went through, I experienced for myself something I want you to be aware of if you are facing a trial right now: The Lord Jesus is not far away. He is with you. He loves you, and He is your very present help. He is reaching out to you and cannot fail you!

TODAY'S PRAYER

Lord Jesus, thank You that You are both the God of my mountaintops and the God of my valleys, and thank You that You are always with me in the valleys as a very present help. Help me to rest in You and the healing power of the holy Communion. I believe that even when I don't feel it, You are carrying me all the way through to my healing. Amen.

DAY 77

HE GOES BEFORE YOU

And we know that all things work together for good to those who love God, to those who are the called according to His purpose.

—Romans 8:28

Throughout Justin's time in the hospital, Wendy and I were very conscious of how the Lord Himself protected Justin and saved him from sustaining injuries that could have been much more devastating. In the same way, I want you to know the Lord watches over you and your loved ones. Because He neither slumbers nor sleeps (Ps. 121:4–5 NIV), you can rest in the assurance that even while you sleep, He works the night shift. He will deliver you and keep you from falling (Ps. 56:13). All the devices of the enemy will be confounded, and even if a weapon has been formed against you, it shall not prosper!

You read Anna's story in the last section, but there is actually more. Throughout her harrowing experience, it was clear the Lord was with her. She wrote:

Looking back, had I not gone on this work trip, and had I not been in Dallas, I would not have been operated on by a Christian surgeon who believes that it is Jesus who heals. And had I not been operated on at that time, my numbing paralysis would soon have become too far advanced, and I could have become an invalid from my neck down or the cancer could have killed me.

And had I not paid US$17 to top up the travel insurance provided for this work trip, I would not have had my huge hospital bill, which came up to over US$200,000, borne entirely by the travel insurance company! All this can only be the Lord's doing, and it is marvelous in my eyes (Ps. 118:23). To God be all the glory and praise! Praise Jesus!

Isn't it amazing to see all that the Lord divinely orchestrated for Anna? That included her surgeon, who according to her nurse "happened" to be among the top ten spinal surgeons in America. Anna also shared that even if she had found out about her cancer earlier, she could not have afforded the medical fees to go through the surgery in Singapore, let alone performed by a top surgeon in America. The Lord truly went before her and caused *all* things to work together for her good.

My friend, whatever you might be going through, trust that God's grace is sufficient for you, for His *strength* is made perfect in your weakness (2 Cor. 12:9). The Greek root word used for *strength* is the word *dunamis*, which refers to the miracle-working power of God.[1] You don't have to try to be strong in and of yourself. His miracle-working power is made perfect in your time of weakness. You *will* get through this trial. Not only that, I am believing with you that you will emerge even stronger than before.

TODAY'S THOUGHT

Put your trust in the Lord Jesus. You might feel helpless against that disease or that ballooning medical bill, but don't lose hope. Just as He was working behind the scenes to position Anna at the right place at the right time and cover all her bills, trust that He is working behind the scenes for you.

TODAY'S PRAYER

Lord Jesus, thank You that You are watching intently over me and my loved ones. Thank You that Your miracle-working power is orchestrating all the things in my life to work together for good and according to Your purpose. I believe that no matter what I see in the natural, You have gone before me, and I will emerge stronger and better than ever. Amen.

DAY 78

JESUS COMES TO YOU IN YOUR VALLEY

Then Melchizedek king of Salem brought out bread and wine; he was the priest of God Most High. And he blessed him and said: "Blessed be Abram of God Most High, Possessor of heaven and earth; and blessed be God Most High, who has delivered your enemies into your hand."

—Genesis 14:18–20

I don't know what valley you are in right now, but I want to share a powerful picture in the Bible that I pray will encourage you.

Every time something is mentioned in the Bible for the first time, it is always significant. Do you know where you find the bread and the wine of the Communion mentioned together for the first time? It's there in today's scriptures.

Who is Melchizedek? The Bible tells us that our Lord Jesus is "a priest forever according to the order of Melchizedek" (Heb. 7:17). Many scholars believe he is a pre-incarnate appearance of Christ. But it is clear that Melchizedek is a type of Christ.

Melchizedek was the king of Salem, which means "peace." But Salem means much more than peace. It also means "complete, safe, perfect, whole, and full."[1]

Melchizedek met Abram in the Valley of Shaveh, or the King's Valley

(Gen. 14:17). The King's Valley is actually in the Kidron Valley. *Kidron* in Hebrew is from the word *qadar*, which means "darkness."[2]

Melchizedek wasn't the only person present with Abram. Bera, the king of Sodom, went out to meet Abram before Melchizedek arrived (Gen. 14:2, 17). Bera's name in Hebrew means "son of evil."[3]

I gave you all that background because I want you to see this: *when you are in a place of darkness, your Lord Jesus comes to you, bearing bread and wine.*

You might be asking, "Won't the Communion become something legalistic that I have to do?" Not if you see yourself receiving the bread and the wine from the Lord Jesus Himself. The Communion is not something that you do; you *receive* the Communion just as Abram did.

In your time of darkness, don't forget that the Lord has given you the Communion as a tangible, practical way of remembering all He has done for you and encountering His love. You don't have to handle the situation all by yourself. The Lord is with you, and He wants you to bring Him every fear and every worry. Talk to Him. Whenever I am afraid I like to sing the words from the psalms of David to strengthen myself in the Lord. May you be filled with His strength as you meditate on and worship Him with these words from the psalmist:

> *You are my hiding place; You shall preserve me from trouble; You shall surround me with songs of deliverance. . . . Whenever I am afraid, I will trust in You. (Ps. 32:7; 56:3)*

TODAY'S THOUGHT

Whatever valley you might be in right now, whatever evil you might be faced with, you are not alone. May your eyes be opened to see that the King of peace is with you. The King of completeness, of safety, and of wholeness is with you, and He comes bearing bread and wine for you. He comes to refresh you and to impart to you His shalom.

TODAY'S PRAYER

Lord Jesus, thank You that You are the King of peace who brings me completeness, safety, and wholeness. Thank You that You come to me in the very places of darkness, bearing the bread and wine, reminding me of all You have done for me. I give You my fears and worries and receive Your shalom. Amen.

DAY 79

THROUGH VALLEYS INTO RESTORATION

The Lord *is close to the brokenhearted and saves those who are crushed in spirit.*

—*Psalm 34:18* NIV

In yesterday's reading, Abram was in a valley immediately after he had secured a great victory. You might be fresh from a victory—maybe you just experienced a breakthrough—but very quickly you can find yourself in a valley. This is why we cannot put our confidence in temporal things. Everyone, no matter what successes they have enjoyed, is susceptible to times of darkness in their lives.

In the same way, just because I am a pastor and I teach on the Communion, it does not mean that I am not confronted with challenges. I know the same is true for other pastors as well, so if you can, please keep your pastors and leaders in prayer—you don't know what they might be going through.

Wendy and I went through a difficult period in our lives. A few years after we had our daughter, Jessica, Wendy became pregnant with our second child, and we were looking forward to meeting our baby. Then, nine weeks into her pregnancy, the doctor told us the baby had no heartbeat. I have never seen Wendy cry the way she cried, and I pray I never will again. Our hearts were broken. All we could do was weep.

When we first lost our baby, our pain was too raw, and honestly, it was hard for us to feel faith in our emotions. But like I said, faith is not about emotions. Even though we were crushed, we continued to trust Him.

By faith, we told the Lord, "We don't understand all that happened, but we know You are a good God. We know You are not behind this, and we put our trust in You. We won't give up on Your promises. You love us, and we know You have a child in store for us, and that child will be a champion." We started to partake of the Communion together as we believed God for a baby, and I even decided to ask the Lord for a baby boy.

Today I want you to know that Wendy and I may have lost our baby, but we have also received our restoration. It took some time, but Justin David Prince came along, and what a restoration he is!

Whatever you may have lost, we are believing with you for your restoration.

TODAY'S THOUGHT

If you have lost a child as we have, I want you to know that your child is growing up in heaven. When David's child died, he said, "I will go to him one day, but he cannot return to me" (2 Sam. 12:23 NLT). That's why as far as Wendy and I are concerned, we have two children here on earth and one in heaven. And if you have loved ones who have passed on, don't be discouraged. If they are believers, you will see them again. They have just relocated to a place where there is no sickness, no pain, no adversity, and they are more alive than any of us.

TODAY'S PRAYER

Lord Jesus, thank You that You are in the valleys with me and that You are near to me when my heart is broken and my spirit is crushed. Help me to know in my heart that faith is not about emotions when I walk through the valley. I declare that my trust is in You, and I am believing You for a full restoration of all I have lost. Amen.

DAY 80

WE DON'T HAVE ALL THE ANSWERS

"I will return her vineyards to her and transform the Valley of Trouble into a gateway of hope."

—Hosea 2:15 NLT

Maybe you are going through a difficult valley. Maybe you are disappointed with God because you have lost a loved one or because you have been battling that medical condition year after year.

I want to encourage you not to ask, "Why?" Asking why will only lead you on a downward spiral into depression. Don't ask, "Why did this happen to me?" Don't ask, "Why is my child not healed even though I have trusted You for years?" or "Why is my loved one going through one tragedy after another?"

The fact is, in this fallen world, we don't have all the answers. One day, we will receive our new bodies, where the corruptible will put on incorruption, and the mortal will put on immortality (1 Cor. 15:53). But until then, I recognize that sometimes bad things happen and I don't know *why*.

But what I *do know* is this: God is a good God. He loves us, and He is *never* behind any pain we go through. Our faith in Him is not based on our experiences; it is based on the unchanging, eternal Word of God, which cannot lie.

Even when things didn't go the way you wanted them to, don't remain in your disappointment. The devil wants you to get angry with God and to give up on His promises. But keep believing that God is *for* you and not against you. Even if the enemy has destroyed something in your life, and even if years have been lost as you waited for the manifestation of your healing, or the days of your youth have been stolen from you, keep believing that God can restore to you what you have lost (Joel 2:25; Job 33:25).

My friend, "let us hold fast the confession of our hope without wavering, for He who promised is faithful" (Heb. 10:23). Keep on looking *to* the Lord for your breakthrough. And if you find that you are too tired to believe anymore, I pray that this promise will carry you through:

> *But those who wait on the LORD shall renew their strength; they shall mount up with wings like eagles, they shall run and not be weary, they shall walk and not faint. (Isa. 40:31)*

TODAY'S THOUGHT

We may not have all the answers, but we can have a full assurance that the troubles we sometimes experience in the valleys are not the works of God. When you are in a valley of trouble, keep on believing in the Lord's goodness and love that were demonstrated on the cross for you, and you will see Him open a door of hope to your restoration and healing.

TODAY'S PRAYER

Lord Jesus, thank You that I don't need to have all the answers to my "why" questions about the bad things and pains I face. Thank You that You are a good God who loves me. You are my God who is always for me and never against me. I declare that my hope is in You alone and what You did for me on the cross to secure my healing and restoration. Amen.

DAY 81

FIND FRIENDS WHO CAN CARRY YOU

Then they came to Him, bringing a paralytic who was carried by four men.

—Mark 2:3

Sometimes it is difficult for us to have faith when we are on our own. When you have no strength and no faith, you need others to pull you through. I want to share with you a precious testimony from Audrey, a leader in my church who experienced that for herself.

In the twenty-ninth week of her pregnancy, her water broke and she was admitted to the hospital for bed rest. Friends prayed with her and her husband, encouraged them, and believed with them for the birth of a healthy baby. She and her husband partook of the holy Communion as frequently as they were able to.

In the thirtieth week, baby Jenna was born, weighing 1.5 kg (3.3 lb), thankfully with no major complications. She was able to breathe on her own and all her organs were functioning properly. She gradually progressed from a tiny baby supported by tubes and needles to tube feeding and finally to normal feeding. Audrey's daily commute to the hospital was exhausting, but she was thankful for kingdom friends who kept them in prayer. Many of them partook of the holy Communion on their own as they prayed for Jenna and her parents. After forty days in the hospital, Jenna was finally allowed to go home.

However, Jenna was soon back in the hospital ICU as her heart rate suddenly became critically low and later became too high. Audrey was devastated and by this time was "out of prayer and out of faith." But church leaders and friends kept surrounding them in an environment of faith and prayer even when they kept meeting with setbacks.

During that period, Audrey shared that I preached a fresh message about the Communion in church, and after she heard it, she and her husband persevered and kept partaking of the Communion for baby Jenna until finally she was out of danger. It was an arduous journey, but Jenna went home strong and healthy. Hallelujah! Audrey shared:

> *As I think of how Jesus healed the paralytic based on the faith of the four friends who lowered him through the roof, I thank God we also had these "four friends." Our friends continually prayed for Jenna and encouraged us to press in to claim God's healing and to partake of the holy Communion.*

If you have been dealing with a long, drawn-out medical condition or you are exhausted from caring for a loved one, depression can creep in as the burden gets too heavy for you. My friend, bring your cares to God, knowing He cares about you with deepest affection, and watches over you so very carefully (1 Peter 5:7 AMP). At the same time, I want you to know God never meant for you to function in a vacuum. His heart is for you to be planted in a local church and not forsake "the assembling of ourselves together" but to exhort and encourage one another (Heb. 10:25). The church is not perfect by any means. But we have a perfect Savior who has done a perfect work on the cross, and there is safety, healing, and provision in the house of God.

TODAY'S THOUGHT

One of the tactics of the enemy is to try to take you away from the body of Christ and isolate you. That's what he did to the Gadarene demoniac, who withdrew from society to live among the tombs (Mark 5:1–5). Don't let him do that to you. If you are not planted in a local church, may I encourage you to consider finding one?

TODAY'S PRAYER

Father, thank You that the church is Your idea, that it is the body of Christ and He is the head. Thank You for providing the local church to be a powerful place where I can be surrounded by godly leaders and friends who love and encourage me and help me to come to You. Help me to be planted in the safety, healing, and provision of Your house. Amen.

Proverbs

SECTION XII

PURSUE THE HEALER

And beginning at Moses and all the Prophets, He expounded to them in all the Scriptures the things concerning Himself.

—Luke 24:27

DAY 82

GO FOR JESUS *HIMSELF*

So it was, while they conversed and reasoned, that Jesus Himself drew near and went with them.

—Luke 24:15

I love the fact that of all the words God could have chosen to call this beautiful meal, He chose the word *Communion*. It speaks of the relationship God wants to have with us, the closeness and intimacy He desires to have with us. I know it can be easy to lose sight of that and even see the Communion as a means to an end, especially when you are battling symptoms in your body. But as you continue to come to the Lord's Table, don't just go after the healing and miss the One who prepared the table for you. Pursue the healer and not just the healing. Pursue the blesser and not just the blessing. When you have Him, you have everything.

Today and over the next two readings, I want to encourage you with one of my favorite stories in the New Testament. As we come to the end of this book, I pray that you are not walking away with mere *information* about what the holy Communion is, but you have experienced what the two disciples did on the road to Emmaus when Jesus Himself drew near and walked with them. That journey to Emmaus took place the same day our Lord Jesus rose bodily from the grave. What was so important to the Lord that He would do it on the day of His resurrection?

The resurrected Christ did this:

> *And beginning at Moses and all the Prophets,* He expounded to them in all the Scriptures the things concerning Himself. *(Luke 24:27)*

Later the two disciples said to each other, "*Did not our heart burn within us* while He talked with us on the road, and while He opened the Scriptures to us?" (Luke 24:32).

As a pastor, that is what I endeavor to do every Sunday, and that is what I pray I have accomplished through the pages of this book. I pray that by the grace of God, I have been able to expound to you in the Scriptures, not a list of rules and regulations, not knowledge that puffs up the intellect, but things concerning *Himself.*

I pray that your heart burned within you as you saw Jesus in the Scriptures and you have experienced His deep, personal love for you as never before. I pray that you have felt Jesus *Himself* drawing near to you, lavishing His love on you and imparting to you all you need. And beyond what He can do for you or your loved one, beyond healing for that condition you might have been battling with, I pray that you have had an encounter with the Lord Jesus *Himself.*

TODAY'S THOUGHT

Whatever your need for healing is today, whether it is physical, emotional, or mental, your answer is found in a greater revelation of Jesus Himself. When Jesus is unveiled to you, your heart will burn with love and passion, your body will be renewed, and your mind will be filled with His shalom-peace, joy, and soundness. It is all about Jesus!

TODAY'S PRAYER

Precious Lord Jesus, thank You for showing me Your love and Your heart for me. As I come to Your table today, I come with a heart to draw near to You and to behold Your beauty and Your grace. I thank You that as I commune with You, You are imparting to me all that I need. Always open my eyes, Lord, to see more of You in the Scriptures. Amen.

DAY 83

KNOW HIM THROUGH THE COMMUNION

Then their eyes were opened and they knew Him.

—Luke 24:31

After Jesus' resurrection, even before He appeared to Peter, James, and John, He chose to appear to two disciples on the road to Emmaus. Why?

I believe the Lord was about to go on a journey of restoration. I am so excited about this I can hardly contain myself, because I believe what you are about to read will blow your mind and heal your body as well. I want you to watch the restoration unfolding.

Look with me at what happened in the garden of Eden where the Lord walked with *two*—Adam and Eve:

> *So when the woman saw that the tree was good for food, that it was pleasant to the eyes, and a tree desirable to make one wise,* she took of its fruit and ate. *She also gave to her husband with her, and he ate.* Then the eyes of both of them were opened, and they knew that they were naked. *(Gen. 3:6–7)*

They ate from the Tree of Knowledge of Good and Evil. And their eyes were opened—to their nakedness. Through that act of eating, sin and death entered the world (Rom. 5:12). Man was never meant to have disease, sickness, or pain. Man was never meant to grow old and die. God hates death. This is why He called death an enemy (1 Cor. 15:26). Our Lord Jesus even wept at Lazarus's death (John 11:35).

But look at how God reversed everything through what happened with the *two* disciples at the end of the journey to Emmaus. Sin and death came in through an act of eating, and we are about to see Jesus restore everything that was lost in the garden of Eden, through another act of eating:

> *Now it came to pass, as He sat at the table with them, that* He took bread, blessed and broke it, and gave it to them. *Then their eyes were opened and they knew Him. (Luke 24:30–31)*

While the two disciples were walking with Jesus, their eyes had been restrained and the Lord prevented them from recognizing Him (Luke 24:16). But the moment they took the bread from Jesus, the Bible tells us that "their eyes were opened." But this time, unlike Adam and Eve, their eyes were opened so that "they knew Him." The word *knew* here is the Greek word *epiginosko*, which means "full or intimate knowledge or revelation."[1] When they took the bread and ate it, their eyes were opened to perceive who it really was in their midst—the Messiah they had followed, who had brought healing and restoration to so many, and who had defeated death!

What is this breaking of bread that could cause the two disciples to *know* Jesus? Doesn't this remind you of another time when Jesus took bread, blessed and broke it, and gave it to the disciples, saying, "Take, eat; this is My body" (Matt. 26:26; Mark 14:22)? The resurrected Christ had the holy *Communion* with the two disciples!

TODAY'S THOUGHT

Each time you break bread, may your eyes be opened to *see Jesus*, and may He be made *known* to you. May you become more and more thoroughly acquainted with Him and have a deeper and deeper revelation of His loveliness and perfection. The Communion is all about remembering Him—not His healing, not His miracles, just Jesus *Himself*.

TODAY'S PRAYER

Lord Jesus, thank You that You came and died for me, rose victorious over sin and death, and reversed everything that was lost in the garden of Eden. Thank You that as I partake of the Communion, You are opening my eyes to see deeper revelations of who You are and what You have done that I might truly know You. May Your full restoration continue to unfold in my life. Amen.

DAY 84

PARTAKE OF THE TREE OF LIFE

Now it came to pass, as He sat at the table with them, that He took bread, blessed and broke it, and gave it to them.

—Luke 24:30

In yesterday's reading, I described how the resurrected Christ had the holy Communion with the two disciples. What a divine honor the Lord Jesus has put on the breaking of bread, on this wonderful sacrament He has given to the church. This is why in my church, we receive the Communion every week. That's what the early church did as well. The book of Acts tells us that the disciples "came together to break bread" on "the first day of the week" (Acts 20:7). Shouldn't we emphasize what our Lord Jesus made central?

We saw previously that God made Adam and Eve complete except for one thing: their spiritual eyes were not opened. God wanted their spiritual eyes to be opened by the Tree of Life, but instead they partook of the Tree of Knowledge of Good and Evil, and their eyes were opened to see their nakedness. Their eyes were opened to see their failures and shortcomings, their lack and their inadequacies, their sin and their shame.

But our Lord Jesus was restoring all that was lost in that garden. I believe when He broke bread for the two disciples, He was letting them eat from the Tree of Life, the tree that God had wanted man to eat from. Our Lord Jesus *is* the Tree of Life, and when we partake of His broken body, we are eating from the Tree of Life. That is why the moment the two disciples took the bread, *their eyes were opened*, and they knew the Lord Jesus. The apostle Paul also prayed that our eyes may be opened, that we may see Jesus, that we may truly have a revelation of His love (Eph. 1:17–18; 3:18–19). I had been searching the Scriptures for years to find out more about the Tree of Life and was so excited when the Lord showed me this.

After the two disciples partook of the Tree of Life, I believe something happened to their bodies: they were infused and energized with the resurrection life of Christ. This was why they could rise up that very hour to walk back to Jerusalem (Luke 24:33), covering fourteen miles in one day (Luke 24:13). Today we can rejoice because that same resurrection life flows into our bodies *each time* we partake of the Lord's Supper.

By the way, after Adam and Eve sinned, their hearts became cold with fear, and they hid themselves when they heard the voice of God in the garden (Gen. 3:10). But as the resurrected Christ walked with the two disciples on the road to Emmaus, their hearts burned with love for Jesus (Luke 24:32), and they wanted to stay longer in His presence (Luke 24:29). Our Lord Jesus has restored the relationship with God that was fractured and lost when Adam and Eve fell, and today we don't ever have to be afraid of the Lord. Whatever challenges come our way, we can have the confidence that He is *for* us (Rom. 8:31), and we can come boldly to His throne of grace (Heb. 4:16).

TODAY'S THOUGHT

Adam and Eve ate their way to the curse and, with it, sickness, stress, diseases, pain, and death. You and I get to partake of the Tree of Life whenever we partake of the Lord's Supper and *eat our way to life and health*!

TODAY'S PRAYER

Lord Jesus, thank You for sacrificing Your own body on the cross to become the Tree of Life for me and to free me to live each day without guilt, condemnation, and shame. Thank You that I get to partake of the Tree of Life whenever I partake of the holy Communion and eat my way to life and health. All praise and glory to You! Amen.

DAY 85

IT IS ALL ABOUT JESUS

"He Himself took our infirmities and bore our sicknesses."

—Matthew 8:17

By now, you are probably familiar with Isaiah 53:4, which says, "Surely He has borne our griefs and carried our sorrows." Notice how the author of the gospel of Matthew quoted it in today's scripture.

I love the word *Himself* because it is so personal and so intimate. Surely He Himself took our diseases and our infirmities. It wasn't an angel. Your health and wholeness were too important to Him, so He *Himself* bore your every sickness and disease.

Take some time to meditate on the word *Himself*. Take some time to remember the One who suffered and died for you, the One who took your infirmities and bore your sicknesses so you need not bear them. Jesus *Himself* did it because you are so precious to Him.

Whatever condition the doctors have diagnosed you with, Jesus Himself has taken it upon His own body. Don't focus on looking for healing; focus on the Lord Jesus Himself. Focus on the One "who *Himself* bore our sins in His own body on the tree, that we, having died to sins, might live for righteousness—by whose stripes you were healed" (1 Peter 2:24).

Many times when you seek Him and simply spend time in His presence, your fears and worries just melt away. You find that in His presence there is shalom-peace. There is healing. There is wholeness. And when you look for your symptoms, you find them *no more*. Why? Because you are in the presence of the Healer.

When God told the children of Israel, "I am the Lord who heals you"

(Ex. 15:26), He was introducing Himself as *Jehovah Rapha*. He was not saying, "I will give you healing" or "I will provide you health." He was saying I AM your healing, and I AM your health. When you touch Jesus, you touch healing. He does not give healing as though it were a thing. He gives Himself.

You don't have to seek after healing, provision, and protection. When you have Jesus, you have all you need. If there is an area of death in your body, the Lord says to you, "*I* am the resurrection and the life" (John 11:25). If doctors have told you that you will die young, the Lord says to you, "*I* am your life and the length of your days" (Deut. 30:20). If you have received a negative diagnosis and are fearful, the Lord says to you, "Do not be afraid. *I* am your shield" (Gen. 15:1). If you have been dealing with relapse after relapse and the discouragement is overwhelming you, the Lord declares to you, "*I* am your strength and your song" (Ex. 15:2)!

TODAY'S THOUGHT

Many studies tell you all the things you need to eat and do if you want to live long and stay healthy. I fully agree you *should* make healthy food and lifestyle choices. But when your well-being is dependent on things you need to *do*, you will never be secure. Let your healing and security be based, instead, on someone who never fails, someone who is all-powerful, all-knowing, and best of all, all-loving. That's when you can have security that is unshakable and peace unspeakable.

TODAY'S PRAYER

Precious Lord Jesus, thank You that it was You Yourself who *so* loved me that You took my diseases and infirmities in Your own body on the tree. Thank You that You are *Jehovah Rapha*, the Lord who heals me and restores me to wholeness. I declare that You are my portion and You are all I need. Amen.

DAY 86

LIVE LOVED BY THE SHEPHERD

"I will feed My flock, and I will make them lie down," says the Lord God. "I will seek what was lost and bring back what was driven away, bind up the broken and strengthen what was sick."

—Ezekiel 34:15–16

Whatever you are facing in your life, you don't have to run around trying to meet all your needs. You just need to seek Jesus *Himself.* When you have the person of Jesus, you have all the benefits that come with the person.

Here is one particular aspect of the Lord that I want to draw your attention to.

Throughout the Bible, we see pictures or personifications of God, such as Him being our fortress, our stronghold, and our tower. One of the most frequently used pictures is of God as our Shepherd. And many times we see the imagery of the shepherd and sheep used in the context of healing. For instance, read today's scripture from Ezekiel.

I love my wide-margin Bible because I can write my own notes and commentaries. Next to Isaiah 53:5–6 and 1 Peter 2:24–25, I wrote, "This imagery of Shepherd and flock promotes healing." Let me show you something really powerful when you compare these two Scripture passages:

> *But He was wounded for our transgressions, He was bruised for our iniquities; the chastisement for our peace was upon Him,* and by His stripes we are healed. All we like sheep have gone astray; *we have turned, every one, to his own way; and the LORD has laid on Him the iniquity of us all. (Isa. 53:5–6)*

> *Who Himself bore our sins in His own body on the tree, that we, having died to sins, might live for righteousness*—by whose stripes you were healed. For you were like sheep going astray, but have now returned to the Shepherd and Overseer of your souls. *(1 Peter 2:24–25)*

During my time of study, I felt the Lord say to me, "The day My people really see Me as their Shepherd, and not just know it in their heads, but experience Me as their Shepherd, their days of sickness are over." We were like sheep going astray, and that's why we were sick. But we have *now returned to the Shepherd and Overseer of our souls.* And because of that, we can have full assurance that by His stripes, we are healed.

By the way, the word for *returned* in the original Greek text is in the passive voice.[1] This means you are not the active agent here. It is the Holy Spirit who has brought you back and returned you. Do you remember the parable our Lord Jesus told about the shepherd who left the ninety-nine sheep to look for the one that was lost (Luke 15:1–7)? The Shepherd is the One who looks for the lost sheep, finds it, and lays it on His shoulder, rejoicing. Our part as sheep is to *simply consent to be loved by Him*, let Him carry us on His shoulders, and rest in His strength.

TODAY'S THOUGHT

Beloved, the safest place you can be today is on the shoulders of your loving Shepherd, far above every sickness and disease.

Whatever condition you have today, know that He was beaten and scourged for you, and receive your healing and wholeness from Him. He has paid the price for your total healing. By His stripes you are healed.

TODAY'S PRAYER

Lord Jesus, thank You that You have made a way for me to return to You, the Shepherd of my soul. Thank You that by the stripes You bore for me, I can rest assured that my days of sickness are over. I gladly consent to live loved by You, to be carried on Your shoulders, and to rest in Your strength. Amen.

DAY 87

ALL YOUR NEEDS SUPPLIED

The Lord is my shepherd;
I shall not want.

—Psalm 23:1

Another well-known picture of God as our Shepherd and healer is articulated in the beautiful Psalm 23. It was written by David, a shepherd who saw the Lord as his Shepherd. Take a moment and read the psalm for yourself in your Bible.

When you see the Lord as your Shepherd, you will not lack, and that includes not lacking for health. Whatever needs you have, you will not lack because your Good Shepherd provides. You don't have to run yourself ragged trying to take care of everything and live as though you have no God. Whatever medical condition you are faced with, stay close to the Shepherd, and allow Him to provide for you.

And did you notice the first thing the Shepherd does? The psalmist wrote, "He makes me to *lie down* in green pastures" (Ps. 23:2). When you allow Him to be your Good Shepherd, He will bring you to green pastures and make you lie down. You can rest, for He will provide for you. He will lead you beside still waters where you can drink and be refreshed. The Hebrew word for *still* is *manuka*, which means "rest."[1] He wants you in a place of resting in the victory He has already won at the cross.

It is not by coincidence that many of Jesus' healing miracles took place on the Sabbath. He healed a man with a withered hand (Matt. 12:10–13), a woman bowed down for eighteen years (Luke 13:10–13), a man with dropsy (Luke 14:2–4), and another man with a thirty-eight-year infirmity at the pool of Bethesda (John 5:2–9), all on the Sabbath. God told His people to observe the Sabbath as a day of rest (Ex. 20:8–11). When we rest, God works; when we work, God rests. I don't know about you, but I can't afford not to have God working in every area in my life!

Maybe you or your loved ones have been dealing with a chronic condition. Allow me to explain that "rest" doesn't mean you don't do what your doctors have advised or don't carry out the physiotherapy exercises prescribed to you, and you simply sit at home in denial. Rest is *not* inactivity; it is Spirit-directed activity where you allow the Holy Spirit to lead you in what to do, and you do it without worrying because you know He is in control.

Do you want to know the result of allowing the Lord to give us rest? Let me show you what King Solomon said:

> *But now the Lord my God has given me rest on every side; there is neither adversary nor evil occurrence. (1 Kings 5:4)*

Don't you love that? I pray that you will experience that in Jesus' name—to come to a place where there is neither adversary nor evil occurrence in your life. Amen!

TODAY'S THOUGHT

Beloved, you don't have to try to handle everything, to look out for yourself, and to be in control of everything in your life. God never meant for you to be your own savior. God is our Good Shepherd, and He wants you to live life loved by Him, knowing that He watches over you. Whatever you face, you can fear no evil, for your Shepherd *is* with you.

TODAY'S PRAYER

Lord Jesus, thank You that You are my Good Shepherd and healer who watches over me and provides for all my needs. Thank You that You make me lie down in green pastures to rest in the victory that You have already won at the cross. I believe You will give me rest on every side and protect me against adversaries and evil occurrences. Amen.

DAY 88

BROUGHT BACK TO LIFE

Yea, though I walk through the valley of the
shadow of death,
I will fear no evil;
for You are with me.

—Psalm 23:4

The psalmist David says that we need not fear any evil, even if we walk through the valley of the shadow of death, for our Good Shepherd *is* with us. Some years ago, I saw for myself how the Lord brought someone through the valley of the shadow of death and literally brought her back from death to life through the holy Communion.

For years we had been organizing trips to Israel for the people in our church. One day we were informed there had been an emergency. One of the ladies from our church had just landed in Tel Aviv. As she was disembarking from the plane, she suddenly collapsed and started foaming at the mouth. An ambulance was immediately dispatched, but on the way to the Assaf Harofeh Medical Center, she suffered a cardiac arrest and her heart stopped. At the hospital, the doctors tried to save her, but there was no response and they almost gave up. Fortunately, they managed to resuscitate her. They were only able to keep her alive through life support, however, and her condition remained critical.

Her doctors diagnosed her with deep vein thrombosis, a rare condition that develops when a blood clot is formed in a vein deep in the body. During the flight, a clot had formed in her leg, traveled to her heart, and finally to one of her lungs. They warned that she would not be able to survive, and even if she did, her brain had been deprived of oxygen for too long. Her doctors monitored her closely, fearing her condition would deteriorate even further.

The lady's husband and some of her family members who were with her prayed over her and partook of the Communion, declaring health and wholeness over her. The church leaders in charge of her tour group also prayed over her.

Meanwhile, my pastors and I were elsewhere in Israel, and by the time we got to the hospital, her face was all bloated and she was hooked up to various tubes and medical instruments. One of my pastors shared with me later that she was in such a dismal condition that he could not look at her. He had to close his eyes when he prayed for her. In the natural, it was really hard to believe she would recover. But by faith, we partook of the Communion in the intensive care unit together with her family and declared that, by the broken body of our Lord Jesus, life was being released into her.

The very next day, she regained consciousness. And her doctors could not find any trace of a clot. They could not understand where the clot had gone. They called her recovery a "miracle" and insisted on keeping her under observation for a few days. But we knew what had happened. Our Lord Jesus had healed her and removed the clot!

TODAY'S THOUGHT

Guess what the lady did when she was discharged from the hospital? She joined the next tour group from our church, and the first place she visited was the Garden Tomb, the place where our Lord Jesus was raised from the dead. Hallelujah! Today, whatever you are facing, His victory over death is also yours.

TODAY'S PRAYER

Lord Jesus, thank You that You walk with me through all the valleys of sickness, disease, injury, pain, and even the shadow of death. Thank You for the provision of the holy Communion that allows me to partake of Your broken body and shed blood. I thank You that You keep meeting with me in the Communion meal and keep flooding my life with Your life and restoring my health. Amen.

DAY 89
THE BEST THAT HEAVEN HAS

"Do not fear, little flock, for it is your Father's good pleasure to give you the kingdom."

—Luke 12:32

Our Lord Jesus went into a synagogue on the Sabbath, and a man was there with a withered hand. The Pharisees were looking for opportunities to accuse Jesus of wrongdoing, so they challenged Him, saying, "Is it lawful to heal on the Sabbath?" Our Lord answered, "What man is there among you who has one sheep, and if it falls into a pit on the Sabbath, will not lay hold of it and lift it out? Of how much more value then is a man than a sheep? Therefore it is lawful to do good on the Sabbath." Then He said to the man, "Stretch out your hand," and restored it as whole as the other (Matt. 12:9–13).

This is what I want you to know: when someone is sick, the Lord never faults and condemns the person. He sees the person as a sheep that has fallen into a pit and needs rescuing. If you are dealing with a medical condition, don't allow the accuser to disqualify you from receiving your healing by telling you things like, "You should have watched your diet" or "You should have exercised more." Even if you were at fault, the Lord Jesus can heal you, and He is most willing to.

That doesn't mean you neglect wisdom in taking care of your health. If you allow Him to, the Lord can lead you even in practical matters like what to eat and how to exercise. The key here is not to pay attention to the voice of shame, condemnation, and accusation. Listen instead to the voice of your Shepherd coming to rescue you!

Our Good Shepherd says He gives His life for the sheep (John 10:11). But do you know the context of this verse? Let me show you:

> *"The thief does not come except to steal, and to kill, and to destroy. I have come that they may have life, and that they may have it more abundantly. I am the good shepherd. The good shepherd gives His life for the sheep." (John 10:10–11)*

Even though He is our Shepherd, He laid down His life as the Lamb of God. Revelation 5:12 declares, "Worthy is the *Lamb* who was slain." Why does God use the picture of the Lamb and not the Shepherd in the sacrifice? Because God wants you to see that Jesus died in your place. He, the Good Shepherd, became the Lamb of God for you. You can have life more abundantly not because you deserve it but because He gave His life for yours. He took your sicknesses and your pains and gave you His wholeness and His health.

Today hear your Lord Jesus saying to you, "Do not fear, for it is your Father's good pleasure to give you the kingdom." Whatever condition you might be faced with, you can believe you will see the full manifestation of your healing. Keep partaking of the Tree of Life through the holy Communion and allow His abundant life to flood your body each time you partake.

TODAY'S THOUGHT

God has already given you the best that heaven has—the Lord Jesus Himself. How will He not with Jesus also *freely give you all things* (Rom. 8:32)? Whatever you might be facing, do not lose heart. You will "see the goodness of the Lord in the land of the living" (Ps. 27:13)!

TODAY'S PRAYER

Father God, thank You that You gave me the very best that You have, the Lord Jesus Himself, to be the worthy Lamb that was slain in my place. Thank You that He took my sicknesses and pains and gives me wholeness and health. I believe and declare that through the holy Communion I will see the full manifestation of my healing and abundance of life. In Jesus' name, amen.

DAY 90

LET'S PARTAKE

Jesus took bread, blessed and broke it, and gave it to them and said, "Take, eat; this is My body." Then He took the cup, and when He had given thanks He gave it to them, and they all drank from it. And He said to them, "This is My blood of the new covenant, which is shed for many."

—Mark 14:22–24

I pray this book has strengthened and encouraged you, and that you now know beyond the shadow of a doubt that God wants you and your loved ones healed and well. I also hope you have learned how you can come boldly to His table and eat and drink of the Lord's supernatural healing, health, wholeness, and life through the holy Communion.

You can partake of the holy Communion by yourself. But I want to encourage you to partake of the Communion together with your family or with like-minded believers who can surround you with faith, especially when you have no strength to believe for yourself. When you gather in His name, He promised in His Word that He will be in your midst (Matt. 18:20). Don't take this journey alone.

For now, as I close these readings, would you give me the privilege of partaking of the Communion together with you? Please prepare the elements of the Communion, and when you are ready, read on.

Let's hold the bread in our hands and talk to our Healer, who paid the price for our health and wholeness at the cross of Calvary:

Dear Lord Jesus, we come to You, and we remember all that You have done for us on the cross. Thank You for loving us so much You gave up heaven for us. Thank You for allowing Your body to be broken so that ours might be whole. As we partake, we receive Your resurrection life, health, and strength. By Your grace, we shall be completely strong and healthy all the days of our lives. Our eyes shall not grow dim, nor shall our strength be abated. No sickness can remain in our bodies because the same power that raised You from the grave flows through us. By Your stripes, we are healed.

Let's partake of the bread.

Now hold the cup in your hands and tell Him:

Lord Jesus, thank You for Your precious blood. Thank You for washing us clean of all our sins. We stand before You completely righteous and forgiven. Your blood has redeemed us from every curse, and today we can freely receive all the blessings that crown the head of the righteous!

Let's drink.

Right now, I believe you are already stronger and healthier. Hallelujah!

My friend, I am looking forward to hearing from you when you receive your breakthrough. When that happens, please write to me at JosephPrince.com/eat so that together we can encourage others who are still trusting God for the manifestation of their healing!

TODAY'S THOUGHT

I pray that the Lord has already left an indelible deposit in your heart and that you have experienced His personal love for you in a way you never thought possible. May you continue to see in all the Scriptures the things concerning Himself. And may you come to His table often, seizing each opportunity to remember all He has done for you and to proclaim His finished work. I declare that your healthiest, most robust, and most energetic days are ahead of you, in Jesus' name! Amen.

TESTIMONY

Life Back into Unborn Baby After Receiving Communion

My family and I had always wanted another child. But as time went by, I gave up because I was already past forty, and it is not easy for women my age to conceive in the natural.

One day my younger daughter asked me when I would have another child. I said to her, "Let's pray, and God will give us one." That night I couldn't sleep. I did a pregnancy test and realized I was pregnant!

However, during the first check-up with the gynecologist, we were told that our baby had no heartbeat and that it was common for women of my age to produce eggs that were not as healthy as those from younger women. Furthermore, it was not my first time losing a child as I had two miscarriages before. We were told to wait for another week to see if our baby had any heartbeat. If not, I was to undergo a procedure to remove the baby.

WE PRAYED, PARTOOK OF THE HOLY COMMUNION, AND BELIEVED GOD FOR A MIRACLE. . . . MY BABY WAS REVIVED AND STARTED TO GROW AGAIN WHEN WE STARTED TO RECEIVE THE COMMUNION.

By then I had been listening to and translating Pastor Prince's messages for four-and-a-half years. Besides being blessed by his preaching on the grace of God, I was also deeply impacted by his teachings on the holy Communion. Although I have been a

Christian almost all my life, I had never known the true meaning of the holy Communion until I heard Pastor Prince teach on it. During the following week, we prayed, partook of the holy Communion, and believed God for a miracle.

At the next check-up, my baby still had no heartbeat, and I was told to make an appointment for the procedure. I hesitated because I had not worked out our daughters' childcare arrangements with my husband. Thinking I was too heartbroken to proceed, the gynecologist said I could wait another week before going for the procedure.

During this time, we prayed with the girls and told them that we would still get to see the baby in heaven even if he or she was not born. I continued to pray, to partake of the Communion with peace in my heart, and to listen to Pastor Prince's messages.

I went for a third check-up and this time there was a heartbeat! My gynecologist was extremely surprised. I believe my baby was revived and started to grow again when we started to receive the Communion. Our miracle baby boy was born healthy and happy. God is great and faithful!

Amy | Taiwan

NOTES

DAY 6

1. NT: 1252, Joseph Henry Thayer, *Thayer's Greek Lexicon* (electronic database), Seattle, Wash.: Biblesoft, Inc., 2006.

DAY 9

1. NT: 2222, William Edwy Vine, Merrill F. Unger, William White, Jr., *An Expository Dictionary of Biblical Words*, Nashville, Tenn.: Thomas Nelson, 1985.
2. NT: 5315, James Strong, *Biblesoft's New Exhaustive Strong's Numbers and Concordance of the Bible with Expanded Greek-Hebrew Dictionary*, Seattle, Wash.: Biblesoft, Inc. and International Bible Translators, Inc., 2006.
3. NT: 5176, Joseph Henry Thayer, *Thayer's Greek Lexicon* (electronic database).

DAY 12

1. H. Kesselman, S. D. Rosen, S. D. Winegarten, editors, "A Guide to Shechita," Shechita UK, May 2009, https://www.shechitauk.org/wp-content/uploads/2016/02/A_Guide_to_Shechita_2009__01.pdf.
2. T. J. McCrossan, *Bodily Healing and the Atonement* (Tulsa, OK: Kenneth Hagin Ministries, Inc., 1989), http://www.schoolofgreatness.net/wp-content/uploads/2018/08/Kenneth-E-Hagin-Bodily-Healing-and-Atonement.pdf.
3. Flavius Josephus, *The Wars of the Jews* (Overland Park, KS: Digireads Publishing, 2010).

DAY 15

1. OT: 7291: James Strong, *Biblesoft's New Exhaustive Strong's Numbers and Concordance.*

DAY 18

1. Steve Rudd, "The Exodus Route, the Population of the Exodus Jews, the Number of the Exodus, How Many Hebrews Were in the Exodus,"

accessed February 14, 2019, http://www.bible.ca/archeology/bible-archeology-exodus-route-population-of-jews-hebrews.htm.

DAY 24

1. NT: 2222, William Edwy Vine, Merrill F. Unger, William White, Jr., *An Expository Dictionary of Biblical Words*, Nashville, Tenn.: Thomas Nelson, 1985.
2. OT: 3444, Joseph Henry Thayer, Francis Brown, Samuel Rolles Driver, and Charles Augustus Briggs, *The Online Bible Thayer's Greek Lexicon and Brown Driver & Briggs Hebrew Lexicon*. Ontario, Canada: Woodside Bible Fellowship, 1993; Licensed from the Institute for Creation Research.

DAY 33

1. To read encouraging praise reports about the Lord's love and faithfulness, visit https://blog.JosephPrince.com/category/praise-reports/.

DAY 48

1. OT: 5027, James Strong, *Biblesoft's New Exhaustive Strong's Numbers and Concordance of the Bible with Expanded Greek-Hebrew Dictionary.*

DAY 49

1. NT: 40, Joseph Henry Thayer, *Thayer's Greek Lexicon* (electronic database).

DAY 51

1. NT: 2842, Joseph Henry Thayer, *Thayer's Greek Lexicon.*

DAY 52

1. NT: 4372, Joseph Henry Thayer, *Thayer's Greek Lexicon.*

DAY 55

1. OT: 5315, Joseph Henry Thayer, Francis Brown, Samuel Rolles Driver, and Charles Augustus Briggs, *The Online Bible Thayer's Greek Lexicon and Brown Driver & Briggs Hebrew Lexicon.*

DAY 56

1. "What Is Hermatidrosis?," WebMD, last reviewed February 15, 2018, https://www.webmd.com/a-to-z-guides/hematidrosis-hematohidrosis#1.

DAY 66

1. NT: 2168, James Strong, *Biblesoft's New Exhaustive Strong's Numbers and Concordance of the Bible with Expanded Greek-Hebrew Dictionary.*

DAY 71

1. OT: 4832, James Strong, *Biblesoft's New Exhaustive Strong's Numbers and Concordance of the Bible with Expanded Greek-Hebrew Dictionary.*

DAY 72

1. NT: 4982, Joseph Henry Thayer, *Thayer's Greek Lexicon* (electronic database).

DAY 75

1. "The Roman Scourge," Bible History Online, accessed March 4, 2019, https://www.bible-history.com/past/flagrum.html.

DAY 77

1. NT: 1411, James Strong, *Biblesoft's New Exhaustive Strong's Numbers and Concordance of the Bible with Expanded Greek-Hebrew Dictionary.*

DAY 78

1. "Shalem," *The NAS Old Testament Hebrew Lexicon*, accessed March 11, 2019, https://www.biblestudytools.com/lexicons/hebrew/nas/shalem.html.
2. "Qadar," *The NAS Old Testament Hebrew Lexicon.*
3. OT: 1298, Joseph Henry Thayer, Francis Brown, Samuel Rolles Driver, and Charles Augustus Briggs, *The Online Bible Thayer's Greek Lexicon and Brown Driver & Briggs Hebrew Lexicon.*

DAY 83

1. NT: 1921, Joseph Henry Thayer, *Thayer's Greek Lexicon* (electronic database).

DAY 86

1. "1 Peter 2:25," BibleHub, accessed March 18, 2019, https://biblehub.com/text/1_peter/2-25.htm.

DAY 87

1. OT: 4496, Joseph Henry Thayer, Francis Brown, Samuel Rolles Driver, and Charles Augustus Briggs, *The Online Bible Thayer's Greek Lexicon and Brown Driver & Briggs Hebrew Lexicon.*

SPECIAL APPRECIATION

Special thanks and appreciation to all who have sent in their testimonies and praise reports to us. Kindly note that all testimonies are received in good faith and have been shared only with the consent of the testimony writers. Each testimony has been edited only for brevity and fluency. Names have been changed to protect the writers' privacy.

MEDICAL DISCLAIMER

This book is not meant to take the place of professional medical advice. If you or your loved one has a health concern or an existing medical condition, please do consult a qualified medical practitioner or health-care provider. We would also advise you to ask and seek the Lord always for His wisdom and guidance regarding your specific health or medical issue, and to exercise godly wisdom in the management of your own physical, mental, and emotional well-being. Do not, on your own accord, disregard any professional medical advice or diagnosis. Please also do not take what has been shared in this book as permission or encouragement to stop taking your medication or stop going for medical treatment. While we make no guarantees and recognize that different individuals experience different results, we continue to stand in faith to believe and affirm God's Word and healing promises with all who believe.

SALVATION PRAYER

If you would like to receive all that Jesus has done for you and make Him your Lord and Savior, please pray this prayer:

> *Lord Jesus, thank You for loving me and dying for me on the cross. Your precious blood washes me clean of every sin. You are my Lord and my Savior, now and forever. I believe You rose from the dead and that You are alive today. Because of Your finished work, I am now a beloved child of God and heaven is my home. Thank You for giving me eternal life and filling my heart with Your peace and joy. Amen.*

WE WOULD LIKE TO HEAR FROM YOU

If you have prayed the salvation prayer or if you have a testimony to share after reading this book, please send it to us via JosephPrince.com/testimony.

STAY CONNECTED WITH JOSEPH

Connect with Joseph through these social media channels and receive daily inspirational teachings:

Facebook.com/JosephPrince
Twitter.com/JosephPrince
Youtube.com/JosephPrinceOnline
Instagram: @JosephPrince

FREE DAILY E-MAIL DEVOTIONAL

Sign up for Joseph's free daily e-mail devotional at
JosephPrince.com/meditate
and receive bite-size inspirations to help you grow in grace.

BOOKS BY JOSEPH PRINCE

Eat Your Way to Life and Health

Come boldly to the Lord's Table and receive your healing! Through engaging Bible-based teaching, Joseph Prince unpacks revelation upon revelation about the holy Communion, and shows you why it is God's ordained way to release life, health, and healing to your body. Get answers to pertinent questions such as if it's God's will to heal you, and be encouraged by testimonies from those who have been healed through partaking of the Communion. Whatever your health challenge, don't give up. He has made a way for you to eat your way to life and health!

Anchored—A 28-Day Devotional

Loneliness. Inadequacy. Fear. Shame. The crushing weight of anxiety. These are storms we've all faced, storms that often threaten to engulf us. But the Lord says we can live anchored in His perfect love, grace, and righteousness through them all. Discover how in this devotional that features twenty-eight easy-to-read thoughts, weekly reflection prompts, free group-activity facilitation resources, and powerful prayer declarations. Enjoy this four-week journey on your own with the Lord, or with your family and friends! Joseph's first-ever young-adult resource will help you live anchored in Christ, no matter where you are in life.

Live the Let-Go Life

Live the Let-Go Life is the go-to resource for anyone who wants to find freedom from the stress and anxieties of modern living. Instead of letting stress and all its negative effects rule your life, discover how you can cast all your cares on the One who cares about you like no other, and experience His practical supply for every need. You'll find simple yet powerful truths and tools to help you get rid of worry and anxiety and experience greater health and well-being. Learn how you can tune in to God's peace, walk daily in His unforced rhythm of grace, and find yourself living healthier, happier, and having time for the important things in life!

The Power of Right Believing

Experience transformation, breakthroughs, and freedom today through the power of right believing! This book offers seven practical and powerful keys that will help you find freedom from all fears, guilt, and addictions. See these keys come alive in the many precious testimonies you will read from people around the world who have experienced breakthroughs and liberty from all kinds of bondages. Win the battle for your mind through understanding the powerful truths of God's Word, and begin a journey of victorious living and unshakable confidence in God's love for you!

Destined to Reign

This pivotal and quintessential book on the grace of God will change your life forever! Join Joseph Prince as he unlocks foundational truths to understanding God's grace and how it alone sets you free to experience victory over every adversity, lack, and destructive habit that is limiting you today. Be uplifted and refreshed as you discover how reigning in life is all about Jesus and what He has already done for you. Start experiencing the success, wholeness, and victory that you were destined to enjoy!

ABOUT THE AUTHOR

Joseph Prince is a leading voice in proclaiming the gospel of grace to a whole new generation of believers and leaders. He is the senior pastor of New Creation Church in Singapore, a vibrant and dynamic church with a congregation of more than thirty-three thousand attendees. He separately heads Joseph Prince Ministries, a television and media broadcast ministry that is reaching the world with the good news about Jesus' finished work. Joseph is also the bestselling author of *The Power of Right Believing* and *Destined to Reign* and a highly sought-after conference speaker. For more information about his other inspiring resources and his latest audio and video messages, visit JosephPrince.com.